Criminal Procedure Demystified in Easy Language

Hendrik Hartzenberg

To Iminje

Table of Contents

Introduction: 4
1. Right to a fair trial 8
2. Trial 9
3. Speedy trial 16
4. Trial by Jury 18
5. The right to counsel 20
6. Presumption of Innocence 28
7. The exclusionary rule 32
8. Self-incrimination 37
9. Double jeopardy 40
10. Bail 48
11. Appeal 55
12. Conviction 64
13. Acquittal 69
14. Mandatory sentencing 73
15. Suspended sentence 77
16. Custodial sentence 82
17. Periodic detention 87

18. Discharge sentence 91
19. Sentencing Rules and Guidelines 95
20. Guilt in Criminal Law 100
21. Totality Principle 105
22. Dangerous offender 109
23. Capital punishment 114
24. Execution warrant 120
25. Cruel and unusual punishment 124
26. Imprisonment 129
27. Life imprisonment 135
28. Indefinite imprisonment 140
29. The "Three Strikes Law" 145
30. Parole 149
31. Probation 155
32. Life in Prison in England, including Wales. 160
33. Criminal Justice 166
34. Habitual Offender 173
35. Miscarriage of Justice 178
36. Pardon 184
37. Recidivism 189
39. Restorative Justice 201
40. Sex Offender Registry 204
41. Sexually violent predator laws 209
42. Exoneration 213
Works Cited 222

Introduction:

Dear Readers,

Welcome to "Criminal Procedure Demystified in Easy Language."

I am privileged to embark on this fascinating journey with you as we explore the interesting world of criminal procedure together. This book was created with all kinds of readers in mind, to break down complicated legal concepts into simple, understandable language. Anyone interested in law will be able to use this book.

My goal is for the book to be as interesting, educational, and informative as possible. Each chapter is carefully written to give you clarity and insight, giving you the knowledge and confidence to understand the basic rules of our justice system.

You should be able to read through this book within a week or two. If you are a student, you can do so before you start the new semester at your university. Every citizen should know what is written in this book. You might get into difficult situations where knowledge about civil procedure law can be valuable to you.

I'm glad you picked this book. I hope you enjoy reading it and that you might benefit from it.

Kind regards,

Hendrik

Criminal procedure is a fundamental principle that ensures fair treatment through the normal judicial system. It encompasses a series of legal rights and procedures that safeguard individuals against arbitrary denial of life, liberty, or property. Key components of the criminal procedure include the right to a fair trial, the presumption of innocence, and protections against self-incrimination and double jeopardy. These principles are not just theoretical but are enshrined in various legal protections and procedural rules.

At the heart of criminal procedure is the right to a fair trial, which guarantees that an impartial tribunal gives individuals a fair and public hearing. This right is closely linked with the right to a speedy trial, ensuring that justice is administered without unnecessary delays. Additionally, the right to trial by jury allows peers to determine the guilt or innocence of the accused, reflecting community values in the justice process.

Legal representation is another cornerstone, with the right to counsel ensuring that defendants have access to legal expertise to navigate the complexities of the law. The presumption of innocence places the burden of proof on the prosecution, ensuring that individuals are considered innocent until proven guilty beyond a reasonable doubt.

Criminal procedure also involves specific procedural safeguards, such as the exclusionary rule, which prohibits the use of illegally obtained evidence in court. Protections against self-incrimination prevent individuals from being forced to testify against themselves, while the principle of double jeopardy ensures that one cannot be tried twice for the same offence.

Bail provisions offer a means for defendants to be released from custody while awaiting trial, balancing the need for public safety with the rights of the accused. Following a trial, the processes of appeal and potential acquittal or conviction (verdict) further ensure that justice is both fair and thorough.

Sentencing is another critical phase where criminal procedure plays a role, from mandatory sentencing and custodial sentences to more lenient options like suspended sentences and periodic detention. Sentencing guidelines and rules aim to promote consistency and fairness in punishment, guided by principles such as the totality principle, which considers the overall impact of the sentence.

Special considerations are given to dangerous offenders and issues like capital punishment, where the stakes are highest. Protections against cruel and unusual punishment underscore the humane treatment of all individuals within the justice system.

The journey through the criminal justice system does not end with sentencing. Mechanisms like parole, probation, and potential pardon offer pathways for rehabilitation and reintegration into society, while the treatment of habitual offenders seeks to address patterns of criminal behaviour.

Ultimately, criminal procedure is integral to preventing miscarriages of justice and promoting restorative justice. It ensures that even those labelled as sex offenders or sexually violent predators are treated with fairness and humanity. The possibility of exoneration remains a testament to the system's commitment to justice and rectifying wrongs.

In summary, criminal procedure embodies the ideals of fairness, justice, and respect for individual rights, forming the backbone of a just and equitable criminal justice system.

1. Right to a fair trial

As an essential principle of justice, the right to a fair trial is upheld by numerous legal systems and international human rights agreements. Perhaps you disagree, but I think most people would prefer it if everyone had a fair trial if necessary. The following are some key points:

There has to be a neutral and impartial tribunal that oversees the trial. As a result, the judges and jurors must be completely objective.

While it is true that public hearings should be held whenever possible to increase transparency and accountability in the judicial system, there may be exceptions to this norm where protecting individuals' privacy, national security, or extreme vulnerability is at stake. Some people need special protection during trials, like children and witnesses.

Defendants have the right to present their case, which may involve presenting evidence and naming witnesses, during a fair trial.

According to the Presumption of Innocence, the accused is thought to be innocent unless proven guilty. "Beyond a reasonable doubt" is the standard of proof, meaning the prosecution has the burden of proof.

Anyone facing criminal charges has the right to legal representation, and in cases where the accused cannot afford it, the state may step in to cover the costs.

Accused individuals have the right to receive complete and timely communication regarding the nature and specifics of the charges against them.

To prevent unfair detention and uncertainty, the right to a swift trial stipulates that the trial must not take an excessive period. Trials can be very nerve-racking and some individuals suffer a lot because of this.

To prevent double jeopardy, a person cannot face further prosecution for the same offence after a verdict of not guilty or guilty has been rendered.

It is within the accused's rights to request a review of their conviction and/or sentence by a higher court.

Article 14 of the International Covenant on Civil and Political Rights and Article 10 of the Universal Declaration of Human Rights are two examples of international texts that embody similar ideas.

2. Trial

In law, a trial is when both sides of a dispute get together to show evidence and information in a tribunal or court, which is a formal place with the power to decide on claims or disputes. The goal of the panel, which can be a judge, a jury, or another named fact finder, is to settle their disagreement.

The trial is in front of a group of people from the community. This is called a jury hearing. If there is only one judge in the case, it is called a bench trial or hearing.

A hearing in front of an administrative body may be a lot like a trial in court, but people don't usually call them cases. Also, an appeal (also called an "appellate proceeding") is not usually the same as a trial because it only looks over the evidence that was given in the trial court and doesn't allow new evidence to be brought in.

The two main trial systems within which trials are conducted.

Adversarial system (accusatory system)

Common law systems typically employ an adversarial or accusatory approach when determining guilt or innocence. It is commonly believed that the truth is more likely to surface through the open competition between the prosecution and the defence, as they present evidence and make legal arguments. The judge plays the role of a neutral referee and ensures that the law is upheld. In certain jurisdictions, particularly in more significant cases, a jury is responsible for determining the facts. However, it is worth noting that some common law jurisdictions have done away with the jury trial (I think juries will not be unaffected by social media being present all the time).

This presents a situation where the competitors are strongly divided, each pursuing their self-interest and intentionally presenting the facts and legal interpretations in a biased manner. The goal is for both sides to engage in a rigorous process of presenting and challenging evidence and arguments, allowing for a thorough examination of their truthfulness, relevancy, and sufficiency. Ensuring fairness, there exists a presumption of innocence, with the burden of proof resting on the prosecution. Sceptics of the system contend that the pursuit of victory takes precedence over the quest for truth. Defendants who have sufficient resources can retain the services of the best legal representation.

Inquisitorial system

In civil law legal systems, the task of overseeing the police investigation into potential crimes is entrusted to an examining magistrate or judge, who subsequently presides over the trial. It is commonly believed that a thorough and unbiased investigation, conducted before and during the trial, is more likely to uncover the truth. The examining magistrate or judge assumes the role of an investigator, guiding the process of gathering facts through the questioning of witnesses, interrogating the suspect, and collecting additional evidence. Lawyers who advocate for the state and the accused have a specific role in providing legal arguments and presenting different interpretations of the facts that arise during the proceedings.

It is expected that all parties involved will cooperate in the investigation by responding to the questions of the magistrate or judge and providing any pertinent evidence when requested.

The trial occurs once all the evidence has been gathered and the investigation has concluded. Therefore, the majority of the factual uncertainties will have already been resolved, and the examining magistrate or judge will have already determined that there is sufficient evidence of guilt. Some critics contend that there may be an imbalance of power when the examining magistrate or judge is tasked with both investigating and adjudicating on the merits of the case. While lay assessors do serve as a type of jury to guide the magistrate or judge after the trial, their role is secondary. In addition, when a skilled professional oversees every aspect of the case until the trial concludes, there are fewer chances to contest the conviction based on procedural errors.

Sorts of Trial

There are also different types of trials based on the kind of disagreement.

Criminal Trials

The purpose of a criminal trial is to settle charges made against a defendant (often by the government). The majority of criminal defendants in common law regimes are entitled to a jury trial. The rights granted to criminal defendants by the state are generally extensive. Criminal trials are governed by the laws of the criminal process.

Civil Trials

Most of the time, a civil trial is used to settle civil claims or lawsuits, which are not criminal issues. There are rules for civil trials in the rules of civil process that won't be discussed here.

Administrative Hearings

Even though administrative meetings aren't usually thought of as trials, they have a lot of the same parts that more "formal" trials do. Administrative law and, to some extent, civil trial law govern the kinds of disputes that are heard in these meetings.

Labour Trials

Labour law, also referred to as employment law, encompasses a comprehensive set of laws, administrative rulings, and precedents that pertain to the legal rights and limitations of working individuals and their organisations (workplaces). It plays a crucial role in resolving various issues that arise between trade unions/labour unions, employers, and employees. Labour law deals with the complex dynamics between employees, employers, and unions, and also focuses on the rights of employees in the workplace and those under employment contracts.

Mistrial

A judge can throw out a trial before the decision is returned. This is called a "mistrial" in the legal world.

A judge can throw out a hearing because:

The court doesn't have the power to hear a case.

Evidence being admitted wrongly or the discovery of new evidence that could significantly change the result of the trial.

Misconduct by a party, a jury, or someone from the outside, that interferes with due process.

A hung jury means that the members of the jury cannot agree on a decision. When there is a criminal trial, if the jurors can't decide on some charges but not others, the prosecution can choose to retry the defendant on the charges that caused the deadlock.

Getting rid of a juror after they have been chosen if there isn't another juror available and the parties don't agree to go ahead with the surviving jurors or if there aren't enough jurors for the trial.

The death or illness of a judge or lawyer on the jury.

Trying to change a plea while a trial is still going on, which is not usually allowed.

A request for a mistrial can be made by either side, and sometimes the judge in charge will declare one on their own motion. If there is a mistrial, the case can be tried again by either the plaintiff or the prosecutors, as long as they are not afraid of being tried again for the same crime.

Brought to trial

"Brought to trial" usually means to set up a court date for a case or to bring a suspect to court. The law, on the other hand, uses it in several different, unclear ways. To bring to trial can also mean to bring a suspect to court while the case is still going on.

Committed for trial in England and Wales

Put in jail or given bail by a magistrates' court under section 6 of the Magistrates' Courts Act 1980, or by any judge or other body with the power to do so, so that they can stand trial before a judge and jury.

Sent for trial

Under section 51 or 51A of the Crime and Disorder Act 1998, sent by a magistrates' court to the Crown Court to be tried in England and Wales.

3. Speedy trial

The right to a speedy trial is a human right in criminal law. It says that a government lawyer can't keep putting off the trial of a criminal suspect for no reason. If not, the power to make these kinds of delays would let prosecutors put anyone in jail for any amount of time without a hearing.

The requirement and need for a "speedy trial" causes prosecutors to work hard to build cases in a reasonable amount of time that matches the seriousness and complexity of the crimes suspects are accused of.

Article 6 of the European Convention on Human Rights says that everyone in Europe has the right to a quick trial.

The Assize of Clarendon in 1166, an act of King Henry II, created this right in English law, which says that a judge will be called if one is not available right away. The Magna Carta, which was written in 1215, says that we will not sell, refuse, or stall "just cause" to anyone.

With the Speedy Hearing Clause of the Sixth Amendment to the United States Constitution, people have the right to a quick hearing. The Speedy Trial Act of 1974 tells us how to handle federal charges. It must start within 70 days of when the information or indictment was made or when the defendant first appears in front of a judge in the case that the charge is still being considered, whichever comes first.

Some states may also provide extra rights for quick trials. A clear "speedy trial" clause was added to the Virginia Declaration of Rights by its main author, George Mason, in June 1776.

If there is a speedy trial violation, the case may have to be thrown out. However, based on the circumstances, the state may be able to bring a new criminal charge against a defendant even though there was a speedy trial violation. To negotiate, defendants can give up their right to a quick hearing.

Relevant case to read: Barker v. Wingo, 407 U.S. 514 (1972)

The US Supreme Court case Barker v. Wingo was about the Sixth Amendment to the U.S. Constitution and criminal defendants' right to a speedy trial. The Court said each case must be examined independently to see if the right to a speedy trial has been violated.

4. Trial by Jury

A jury trial, also called a trial by jury, is a court case where the facts and results are decided by the jury. It is different from a (bench) trial with a judge.

In the Roman legal process, some courts were functioning like juries. This is because Roman judges were regular people, not legal experts. Important trials were always held in front of hundreds of "judges" in the centuries Centuriate Assembly. Roman law said that judges had to be chosen once a year. They were to settle disputes by acting as jurors, and a praetor did many of the tasks of a judge. Because they would have a personal interest in the case, high-level government officials and their families were not allowed to be judges. People who had been convicted of major crimes were also not allowed to be judges.

People in many common law legal systems, but not all, go to trial with a jury for most major crimes. Some common law countries have done away with jury trials because they believe jurors can be biased. In the US, jury trials are used in criminal cases and are also common in a wide range of cases that are not criminal. In other common law countries, jury trials are only used in a very small number of civil cases, like suits for malicious prosecution and false imprisonment in England and Wales.

In most other places in the world, there are almost no civil jury trials at all. In some civil law areas, however, there are arbitration panels whose members are not lawyers but do decide cases in certain areas of law that are related to the members' areas of knowledge.

The Role of the Jury

In most places with common law, it is up to the jury to find out what happened, while the judge makes the law. They must hear both sides of a case, judge the evidence, choose the facts, and decide based on the law and the jury's instructions. Most of the time, the judge decides the punishment, while the panel only decides whether the person is guilty or not guilty. A clever prosecutor or lawyer can sometimes manipulate the thoughts of jurors by influencing their emotions.

Waiving the right to a jury trial

People who are being charged can give up their right to a jury hearing in some places, which means they will be tried by a judge instead. Both civil and criminal cases can be tried by a jury in the United States. Offenders in England and Wales are put into three groups: summary, indictable, and either way. For summary offences, there are no jury trials. If a summary offence is also tried with an indictable or either-way offence, the defendant has the right to ask for a trial by jury. The either-way offence is a criminal offence subject to adjudication in either the magistrates' or crown court. If the magistrates determine that their sentencing powers are adequate to address the offence, the defendant may choose between a summarily resolved case in the magistrates' court or a trial by jury in the Crown Court upon indictment.

Two-thirds of jury trials are criminal, while one-third are civil, traffic, family and municipal ordinance, trials. Most criminal cases are handled by a plea deal, which avoids the jury trial, thereby saving time and money.

5. The right to counsel

In most countries in the West, in criminal law, the right to counsel means that a defendant has the legal right to have the help of a lawyer, and if the defendant can't afford a lawyer, the defendant can demand that the government hire a lawyer or pay their fees. The right to a lawyer can be considered part of the right to a fair hearing.

United States of America

Criminal defendants have several rights protected by the Sixth Amendment. One of these is the right to a quick, public hearing by a fair jury made up of people from the state and district where the crime was allegedly committed. The impartial jury requirement says that jurors must not be biased and that the jury must include people from different parts of the community. Often the right to a jury only applies to crimes that are punishable by more than six months in jail.

Using a lawyer without having to pay for services rendered.

Relevant case to read: Gideon v. Wainwright, 372 U.S. 335 (1963)

In the case of Gideon v. Wainwright, the U.S. Supreme Court made a significant ruling. They determined that the Sixth Amendment of the U.S. Constitution mandates that U.S. states must provide lawyers to criminal defendants who cannot afford their own.

The Court concluded that having legal representation is crucial to protect the fundamental human rights of life and liberty, as guaranteed by the Sixth Amendment. The Sixth Amendment serves as a reminder that without these constitutional safeguards, justice cannot be ensured.

A criminal defendant who can't pay for a lawyer has the right to have one chosen for them by the government. The Supreme Court eventually recognised this right, and it now applies in all federal and state criminal cases where the defendant is actually in jail or in case of a felony, faces a sentence of more than one year in prison. In misdemeanour cases, criminal defendants do not have the right to appointed counsel if they are not sentenced to actual imprisonment. The court evaluates the right to counsel on a case-by-case basis for parole revocation.

Regarding federal law on civil proceedings, it is important to note that juveniles in delinquency proceedings have a constitutional right to legal representation. Additionally, prisoners who are involuntarily transferred to a mental health facility have the right to receive qualified and independent assistance. However, this does not necessarily mean they will be provided with an attorney. The provision of appointed counsel is determined on an individual basis. In civil contempt proceedings concerning non-payment of child support, the U.S. Supreme Court has ruled that there is no federal constitutional entitlement to legal representation, even if the individual is facing imprisonment. This is applicable as long as the following conditions are met: a) the state is implementing adequate procedural safeguards to ensure that the person has the means to pay but is deliberately choosing not to do so; b) the case is not exceptionally intricate; and c) the plaintiff is not the government and is not being represented by counsel. Ultimately, every state ensures that individuals have the right to legal representation in certain civil proceedings. These proceedings typically include termination of parental rights, abuse/neglect cases, civil commitment, paternity disputes, and civil contempt matters. The state court decisions may rely on the interpretation of either the federal or state constitution. According to the principles of federalism, a state court has the authority to provide more rights under its state constitution than what the Supreme Court has acknowledged under the federal constitution.

Pro se representation in court

Relevant case to read: Faretta v. California, 422 U.S. 806 (1975)

In the absence of legal representation, you are acting "pro se." We refer to someone who represents himself in court as a "pro se litigant" or "self-represented litigant." The Latin phrase "pro se" means "on one's own behalf," while a "litigant" is a person who files a lawsuit or is sued in court.

A criminal defendant can choose pro se representation during trial provided they so choose knowingly and freely, according to the ruling in Faretta v. California in 1975. Standing counsel is not inherently a violation of this right. The right to self-representation on appeal is not guaranteed under the constitution.

Giving legal information that isn't biassed

Anyone who is being accused has the right to a lawyer who is not involved in any possible conflicts of interest, whether they hire a lawyer or are assigned one.

Ineffective legal help

Relevant case to read: Strickland v. Washington, 466 U.S. 668. (1984)

The Supreme Court set the threshold for evaluating when a criminal defendant's right to counsel under the Sixth Amendment is infringed by that counsel's subpar performance in the famous case of Strickland v. Washington, 466 U.S. 668.

The Court decided in Strickland v. Washington in 1984 that a defendant may be granted relief on collateral review provided they can show that the defence counsel's performance fell short of an objective standard of reasonableness (the "performance prong") and that, but for the poor performance, there is a reasonable chance that the proceeding's outcome would have been different (the "prejudice prong").

A defendant who enters a guilty plea must demonstrate that they would not have done so but for the inadequate performance of their attorney to meet the prejudice prong of Strickland.

Relevant case to read: Padilla v. Kentucky, 559 U.S. 356

The Court ruled in Padilla v. Kentucky in 2010 that counsel's failure to notify an alien pleading guilty of the possibility of deportation fell short of the objective standard of the performance prong of Strickland and allowed an alien who would not have pleaded guilty but for such failure to withdraw his guilty plea.

England, Wales, Scotland and Northern Ireland

The Prisoners' Counsel Act of 1836, gave people in common law states their first right to the professional assistance of a lawyer.

The Legal Aid Agency helps people in England and Wales with their legal problems. They do this for both civil and criminal situations. Legal help in criminal cases is based on a person's income, unless the defendant is 16 or younger, in full-time school, or getting certain benefits. A person who is being accused may be asked to pay for their defence.

In Scotland, civil and criminal legal aid is provided by the Scottish Legal Aid Board. Legal aid is offered in criminal proceedings to persons who are intellectually or physically impaired, hold English as a second or foreign language, are facing significant charges that could result in jail time or a loss of employment, and are awaiting appeals. Legal aid applicants must demonstrate that they are unable to pay for their own legal representation or that doing so would be unjust to them or their families. In civil proceedings, legal assistance is given to applicants who demonstrate that they are unable to cover their legal expenses and to those whose cases are judged to have a solid legal foundation.

Aid in civil and criminal matters is offered by the Legal Services Agency of Northern Ireland. Means-testing applies to civil legal aid. Anyone being questioned by the police is entitled to free criminal legal assistance. Legal assistance for criminal trials is merit- and means-tested to ascertain if providing the defendant with legal help is in the best interests of justice.

France and Germany

In France, when a defendant was tried in the assize courts that decided serious offences, they were required to have legal representation, because these cases can be very complex. This was mandated by the written Napoleonic Code of Criminal Instruction, which was approved in France in 1808 and served as an inspiration for numerous other laws in civil law nations. In France, the right to counsel is wide and it is guaranteed to all criminal defendants, and it also extends to civil and administrative disputes. France has extensive legal help because legal residents of France are eligible for state-funded legal assistance for criminal, civil, and administrative proceedings; in some situations, this funding may also be applied to cases in other European countries. There is a sliding scale of support based on income and eligibility is means-tested. Higher earners are only entitled to have 25% or 55% of their legal fees covered, depending on their income, while those at or below the lowest threshold are entitled to full legal assistance, with all costs covered by the state. A nationwide network of public legal consultation centres in France provides state-funded legal advice. While some centres limit their services to low-income individuals, others provide free legal help to anybody residing there.

In Germany, even if a defendant does not want legal representation, it is required for all those facing charges that carry a minimum one-year jail sentence to have representation from a lawyer. If a defendant does not have legal representation, the court will assign one to represent them. In Germany, there is no formal public defender system. A defendant may designate a particular attorney, and the court may assign any attorney to represent a particular defendant. If found not guilty, the defendant will not be required to pay legal fees; nevertheless, if found guilty, they will be responsible for paying the attorney's fees unless the court determines that the defendant is impoverished. In civil disputes, the state helps those who cannot afford to retain an attorney by offering legal counsel, guidance, and assistance with court fees; however, this assistance is only given when it is determined that the case has a fair prospect of success.

Legal representation in Japan

The right to legal counsel is guaranteed by the Japanese Constitution but in a different way than in most Western countries because you do not always have the right to be represented by counsel. In cases when the defendant is a minor or cannot afford legal representation, the court has the authority to assign one at the defendant's expense. Court-appointed counsel is only entitled to after charges are filed. A duty lawyer is allowed one free visitation after an arrest to provide legal advice, explain the relevant laws and processes, and get in touch with the suspect's family. After that, the suspect is responsible for paying the lawyer for any more services. When being questioned by police, suspects do not have the right to be represented by counsel.

6. Presumption of Innocence

Relevant case to read: Woolmington v DPP [1935] AC 462

The Court was the House of Lords.

The full case name is: Reginald Woolmington v Director for Public Prosecutions

It was decided on the 23rd of May 1935

Legislation cited: Criminal Appeal Act 1907 s. 1

Criminal Appeal Act 1907 s. 4

Criminal Evidence Act 1898

Judges sitting for this case: Viscount Sankey, Lord Atkin, Lord Hewart, Lord Tomlin, and Lord Wright.

This is a very interesting case that you can read and you might have your own opinion about the verdict.

The Latin phrase Ei incumbit probatio qui dicit, non qui negat, which means "the burden of proof is on the one who declares, not on the one who denies," is commonly used to refer to the presumption of innocence.

"Presumption of innocence" is a legal principle that states the burden of proof is on the prosecution, who must show that the defendant is guilty beyond a reasonable doubt. "Presumed innocent until proven guilty" is a common way to put this, and it was first used in a trial at the Old Bailey in 1791 by the British barrister Sir William Garrow (1760–1840). Garrow was adamant that the prosecution's case be vigorously examined in court. 'The golden thread' that appears in English criminal law was later described by the English Court of Appeal in its 1935 judgement of Woolmington v Director of Public Prosecutions. The initial official expression of this was made by Garrow.

In his influential 1760s treatise, Commentaries on the Laws of England, the English lawyer William Blackstone stated if ten guilty people get away with it (a crime), that's better than one innocent person suffering injustice.

It is the idea that a person is presumed innocent unless and until they are proven guilty. Presumption of innocence is a fundamental legal right of the accused in a criminal trial in several countries. The prosecution now has the burden of proof. A sufficient amount of persuasive evidence must be gathered and presented to the jury or judge to establish the accused's guilt beyond a reasonable doubt. The accused will be found not guilty if there is still a reasonable doubt. In criminal proceedings, the accused is deemed innocent under English common law. Similar to breach of contract proceedings, both parties must provide evidence in civil cases. In all legal proceedings, the accused is always considered innocent under Anglo-American Common Law. The onus is always on the accuser to provide proof because the accuser has the burden to prove guilt.

The presumption of innocence is the important legal doctrine in Western countries that holds that a person is innocent unless and until they are proven guilty of a crime. The prosecution has the legal burden of proof under the presumption of innocence, and it is their responsibility to provide the judge or jury with strong relevant evidence. The accused is exonerated and acquitted of all charges if the prosecution cannot prove that the allegations are true. Most of the time, the prosecution has to establish the accused's guilt beyond a reasonable doubt. If a reasonable doubt persists, the defendant must be acquitted meaning the defendant was found not guilty. In a criminal trial, the accused has a legal right known as the presumption of innocence, this is in contrast to a presumption of guilt. Article 11 of the UN's Universal Declaration of Human Rights states that it is also an international human right.

Jean Lemoine originally articulated the presumption of innocence in Latin "quilbet presumitur innocens nisi probetur nocens". In English it means "a person is presumed innocent unless proven guilty ". This is based on the legal inference that the majority of people are not criminals. It wasn't only that the prosecution has the burden of proof in a criminal case; the defendant also deserves certain protections, including as being informed of the accusation in advance, having the ability to face the accuser, having access to legal representation, and more.

The burden of proof is entirely on the state when it comes to the most important aspects of the case. No burden of proof is on the defendant with regard to the case's essential facts.

If the defendant does not want to testify or provide evidence, it cannot be used against them. They are not required to do so, and they are not even required to summon witnesses.

No adverse conclusions should be drawn by the jury or judge from the defendant's presence in court, representation by an attorney, and the fact that they are accused of a crime. All they have is what they heard and saw at trial to make a decision.

7. The exclusionary rule

Most evidence obtained in violation of the US Constitution cannot be used by the government due to the exclusionary rule. Evidence obtained by an unlawful search or seizure in violation of the Fourth Amendment is subject to the exclusionary rule, as decided in Mapp v. Ohio. In most Western countries, no one is exempt from the exclusionary rule; it doesn't matter if they are citizens, legal or illegal immigrants, or tourists. The exclusionary rule is a United States constitutionally-based legal principle and prophylactic rule that forbids the admission into evidence of any evidence that has been obtained or examined in a way that violates the defendant's constitutional rights. The term "prophylactic rule" refers to a set of judicially enacted regulations that go above and beyond what is necessary to preserve a constitutional right, even when the right in question may appear to require less protection.

In the United States, the Fourth, Fifth and Sixth Amendments are very important in dealing with the exclusionary rule. Citizens are meant to be protected from unlawful searches and seizures by the exclusionary rule, which is based on the Fourth Amendment in the Bill of Rights. The exclusionary rule also deter and punish prosecutions of police and prosecutors who violate the Fifth Amendment's prohibition against self-incrimination by unlawfully collecting evidence. The right to counsel, guaranteed by the Sixth Amendment, is further protected by the exclusionary rule.

Purpose and boundaries of the regulation

Purpose

The exclusionary rule is not applicable in hearings concerning the revocation of parole, grand jury proceedings, or civil cases.

When determining whether police activity is illegal for exclusionary rule reasons, the legislation that is in force at the time of the action is important.

Indirect evidence derived from criminal conduct

Evidence derived indirectly from unlawful state activity is also inadmissible, according to the "fruit of the poisonous tree" theory. The government cannot utilise fingerprints collected while a defendant was in jail as evidence, for instance, if the arrest was made without proper authorization. The fingerprints are forbidden since they would not have been collected by the police without the unlawful arrest.

This theory also prohibits the following types of evidence:

When evidence that was unlawfully obtained was the reason for the search and was confiscated during the search.

A plea bargain in which the defendant admits guilt after admitting evidence that was obtained illegally.

Claims based on data obtained through unlawful wiretaps.

Questioning that does not include a Miranda warning, however, is exempt from the "fruit of the poisonous tree" theory. Evidence derived from confessions is acceptable, even though a confession acquired in violation of Miranda is not. The prosecution may still utilise a witness's testimony even if they obtain their identity through a confession that violates Miranda.

Illegally obtained evidence and any legal evidence derived from unlawful searches are both rendered inadmissible in court under the "fruit of the poisonous tree" argument.

Limitations of the exclusionary rule.

Some of the ways the exclusionary rule has been limited are as follows:

Proof that a private individual wrongfully seized evidence from the accused can be used in court under the private search theory. Because the Fourth Amendment applies only to government personnel, the exclusionary rule serves to safeguard citizens' right to privacy.

To have standing to seek suppression of evidence, the unlawful search must have infringed upon the constitutional rights of the individual (the party filing the court application).

Concerning third-party privacy rights, the exclusionary rule is non-applicable. But the "jus tertii" standing exception makes a small exception to this rule. The first exception is when a party can defend itself against government acts by claiming the rights of a third party.

In order to undermine the defendant's credibility during cross-examination, it may be acceptable to use evidence that was obtained illegally, as long as it serves to discourage gamesmanship. For instance, the exclusionary rule cannot be used to defend a criminal who knowingly makes a general statement denying any involvement with drugs. On the other hand, during cross-examination, the government cannot ask too general questions to use inadmissible evidence.

The court case Nix versus Williams established the "inevitable discovery" theory, which states that evidence found during an improper search can be presented in court if it has been found eventually regardless of the search.

The "knock-and-announce" exception allows the admission of evidence gathered by police even when they did not properly knock and announce their presence before searching a residence.

The "silver platter concept" used to be a legal loophole that let states turn over evidence they had illegally collected to the federal government and have it admitted into trial. Elkins v. United States, however, declared the theory to be unlawful in 1960.

Evidence obtained may still be utilised under "the good-faith exception" if law enforcement officials relying on a flawed search warrant are working in good faith (bona fides).

The "independent source doctrine" states that evidence can be admitted into evidence if it is obtained both illegally and via separate, lawful sources.

Attenuation: Even if the evidence loses its direct correlation to the unlawful conduct due to the passage of time or other intervening circumstances, it may still be admitted in court. Evidence gathered during an unlawful stop by police may be acceptable if a valid outstanding arrest warrant is subsequently found.

Conclusion

Many judges have criticised the rule in the past including Judge Benjamin Cardozo but others supported the rule that was already in use in the USA for a long time and that the rule was in harmony with the concept of due process.

8. Self-incrimination

The term "self-incrimination" is used in criminal law to describe when someone makes a statement that could lead to allegation or prosecution for a crime. Direct self-incrimination occurs when someone discloses information about themselves through questioning; indirect self-incrimination occurs when someone discloses information about themselves freely, without external coercion.

Offenders in many jurisdictions are not required to confess unless they voluntarily do so; conversely, they are not penalised for opting not to cooperate with authorities. The right to remain silent and the right to legal counsel are among the legal warnings that suspects are currently being issued in numerous countries and jurisdictions. While not all countries follow these rules exactly, those that are part of the European Union have modelled their legal systems after the EU's.

In England, the privilege to be silent in matters of state was first established in the British Isles. The idea of giving people the tools they need to avoid incriminating themselves has developed into a corpus of legislation in nations whose legal systems are following the tradition of English common law.

According to the Criminal Evidence Act 1898 s1(2) (as modified), defendants in criminal proceedings in England

and Wales currently have the privilege against self-incrimination as mandated by statute:

"The prosecution has the right to ask any witness in a criminal case any question during cross-examination, even if doing so may implicate him in the crime for which he is being tried."

The well-known Criminal Justice and Public Order Act 1994 modified the right to silence for England and Wales. This act allows jurors to draw inferences when a suspect initially refuses to explain something but then explains. Since the defendant declined to give an explanation while police were interviewing him, the jury can reasonably conclude that he later made up the story or the jury can choose not to draw that conclusion, depending on their understanding of the explanation.

Relevant case to read: Miranda v. Arizona (1966)

In the United States of America, the accused are shielded from coercion from having to testify against themselves in a criminal trial under the Fifth Amendment of the US Constitution. Here is the text of the Amendment:

"It is against the law to force an individual to testify against themselves in a criminal prosecution."

A person also has the right to stay silent in order not to divulge any incriminating information while in police custody, as stated in the Miranda verdict. An individual must inform law enforcement officials clearly and unmistakably that they are using their right to remain silent to enforce this constitutional protection. It is important to note that staying silent does not constitute an exercise of this constitutional right unless one expresses it beforehand.

Law enforcement officers are obligated to inform detained suspects of their rights to stay silent and legal representation in accordance with the Fifth Amendment privilege against self-incrimination, as established in Miranda v. Arizona (1966).

Before questioning begins, suspects should be informed of their rights, including the ability to stay silent, the possibility that their statements could be used against them in court, the right to an attorney, and the appointment of an attorney to represent those who cannot afford one. Additionally, the subject is not allowed to willfully waive these warnings and consent to answer questions or make a statement until after they have been delivered and understood.

Furthermore, the Fifth Amendment safeguards particular forms of evidence, namely testimonial evidence, which consists of remarks made under oath by the individual in issue.

Truthful witnesses incriminating themselves.

Relevant case to read: Ohio v. Reiner, 532 U.S. 17 (2001)

No matter how genuine a remark is, it can nonetheless incriminate the speaker even if the speaker is completely innocent if it raises the likelihood that they will be implicated, charged, or punished. Testimony, therefore, can implicate even an innocent witness if the witness is truthful. The Fifth Amendment right has been upheld by the US Supreme Court and ensures the safety of both the innocent and the guilty. The Fifth Amendment serves the fundamental purpose of shielding innocent individuals from being caught in the web of unclear circumstances. The truthful statements made by both innocent and guilty witnesses can offer the government damning evidence against themselves.

9. Double jeopardy

Jurisprudence recognises the double jeopardy defence, which is most common in common law jurisdictions, as a means to avoid retrial on the same or comparable charges after a previous acquittal or conviction, with the exception of extremely rare instances of prosecutorial or judicial misconduct within the same jurisdiction.

While the idea of double jeopardy is prevalent in criminal law, res judicata is comparable in civil law. While the double jeopardy clause in criminal trials prevents repeated prosecutions for the same crime, the same evidence can be used to prosecute a different offence in a subsequent trial. A more robust kind of protection known as "res judicata" bars future claims or actions based on a topic that has already been adjudicated. The peremptory plea is a variant in common law jurisdictions; it might be "autrefois acquit" (meaning "previously acquitted") or "autrefois convict" (meaning "previously convicted"). These ideas seem to have their roots in the larger principle of "non bis in idem" ('not twice against the same'), which had its place in classical Roman law.

The court will normally decide as a preliminary matter whether the plea is supported in cases where a double jeopardy issue is made; if it is, the scheduled trial will not go on. However, some nations may provide specific exceptions. A constitutional right to be free from double jeopardy exists in the United States and other nations. No norm of international law recognises double jeopardy. Except when expressly agreed to in a bilateral contract, as is the case, for instance, in the Schengen Agreement between the European Union and some member states, it does not apply across international borders. Every country has its own perception of double jeopardy, but usually, the idea remains the same or nearly the same.

The Council of Europe

Almost every European country and every EU member has ratified the European Convention on Human Rights, which is required for membership in the Council of Europe. Article 4 of the convention's optional Protocol No. 7 prevents double jeopardy by stating that no one may face further criminal proceedings within the same state for the same offence for which they have already been acquitted or convicted according to that state's laws and penal procedure. Every EU member state has approved this optional treaty except for Germany, the UK, and the Netherlands. But individual member states can pass laws that let you start over with a case if you find fresh evidence or if the last round of procedures had a major flaw. In numerous European nations, the prosecution has the option to appeal acquittals to higher courts if fresh or newly found information is presented, or if there has been a fundamental flaw in the prior processes that could impact the result of the case.

A not-guilty verdict in the Netherlands can be appealed by the state prosecution at the bench. A district court retrial allows for the introduction of new evidence. This means that the same claimed offence can lead to two trials. The defence has the option to appeal a conviction from the district court to the Supreme Court based on procedural grounds. If this complaint is accepted by the supreme court, the matter will be restarted at a different district court. The prosecution may present fresh evidence, yet again.

In France, art. 6 of the Code of Criminal Procedure states that once all appeals have been exhausted, the decision is final and the prosecution's action is concluded unless the final verdict is falsified. No amount of incriminating evidence may prevent a conviction for a crime that has already been decided. Through a process called révision, however, a condemned person might ask for a new trial based on fresh evidence that exonerates them. An acquittal can be appealed by the prosecution under French law.

In Germany, in the event of a final judgement, the German Federal Republic's Basic Law, the Grundgesetz, safeguards against double jeopardy. The lack of an appeal renders a verdict final. According to Art. 103 (3) GG, no one shall be subject to more than one punishment for the same offence under general criminal law.

A verdict in the first instance can be appealed by each trial party. If either the prosecution or the defendants are dissatisfied with a judgment, they have the option to appeal. The second instance court, the Berufungsgericht, re-opens the case, reviews the evidence and reasoning, and then issues a verdict.

Only for formal judicial reasons can a party appeal a decision from the second instance if they are unhappy with it. To determine if all laws were applied appropriately, the case will be reviewed in the third instance, the revisionsgericht.

Since the historical event as a whole is typically thought of as a single sequence of events from which to disentangle it would seem unreasonable, the rule applies to it. This remains accurate regardless of whether more evidence links to other offences.

In the event that the defendant is found guilty or in the following circumstances, the Penal Procedural Code (Strafprozessordnung) permits a retrial, also known as a Wiederaufnahmeverfahren: It is acceptable to get a retrial after a final verdict if the defendant is found not guilty. If a document that was supposed to be authentic during the trial turns out to be fake or falsified, if an authorised expert or witness provided false testimony or deposed incorrectly, if the decision-maker, a professional or lay judge, failed to fulfil their duty as a judge in the case, and if a convicted defendant makes a credible confession either in court or outside of it, then the decision-maker may step in.

When the court orders a summary sentence—a punishment that does not require a trial—for a less serious offence, there is another exemption.

If additional facts or evidence are introduced that, either on their own or in combination with the existing evidence, provide sufficient grounds for a felony conviction, the court may order a retrial in which the defendant is found not guilty following a final order of summary punishment.

Double jeopardy in England.

In England, double jeopardy has evolved considerably in the last several decades. An individual could not be tried twice for the same crime under the old principle of double jeopardy. In England and Wales, however, the Criminal

Justice Act 2003 was amended in 2005, allowing for a retrial in major cases if new and persuasive evidence is discovered. Cases where new forensic procedures, like DNA testing, produced significant evidence that wasn't there in the first trial were major factors in this shift.

Several high-profile cases prompted the UK to change its double jeopardy law. These instances brought to light the shortcomings of the conventional double jeopardy rule and served as a powerful catalyst for judicial change, which ultimately resulted in the creation of exceptions for particularly heinous crimes in cases when fresh and convincing proof is discovered.

The Billy Dunlop Case: In 1989, there was insufficient evidence to convict Billy Dunlop of Julie Hogg's murder in both of his trials. While serving time for a separate crime, he ultimately admitted to the murder. Retrial was not an option due to the double jeopardy law that was in effect during that period. But his case was crucial in showing that reform was necessary. The 2006 conviction of Dunlop followed a retrial following the legislative amendment.

The Case of Stephen Lawrence: In 1993, a Black adolescent named Stephen Lawrence was assassinated in London in an act driven by racial hatred. The accused were found not guilty due to bungled handling of the initial investigation and the trials that followed. New information surfaced following a public outcry and the Macpherson Inquiry's examination. The 2012 retrial and conviction of two of the first suspects were a result of this.

Other significant instances that contributed to the debate over the UK's double jeopardy rule include:

Raymond Carroll was found not guilty of the 1973 infant murder charge owing to a lack of evidence in the R v. Carroll Case, which was significant in the reform debate in the United Kingdom but occurred in Australia. Despite his subsequent confession, a retrial was not possible due to the double jeopardy clause. Many people used this instance to argue that the legislation should be changed.

The 1983 acquittal of John William Burrows in the murder of 20-year-old Annette Waring is known as the Burrows Case. Years later, new DNA evidence surfaced, which could have justified a new trial had the legislation been changed sooner.

Ronald Joseph Lilley was found not guilty of Patricia Grayson's murder in the 1979 case of R v. Lilley. Subsequently, strong evidence connecting him to the crime was produced by new forensic techniques. Retrials supported by fresh, convincing evidence should be made possible through reform, as this case has shown.

The Criminal Justice Act of 2003 in England and Wales was largely shaped by these trials, as well as those of Stephen Lawrence and Billy Dunlop, which led to a substantial reform of the double jeopardy legislation.

Double jeopardy in the United States of America

The United States of America's common law safeguard against double jeopardy is upheld by the Fifth Amendment's Double Jeopardy Clause, which states that no one shall face the death penalty more than once for the same crime. As I just mentioned, the idea of double jeopardy is codified in the United States Constitution in the Fifth Amendment.

Individuals are protected against being tried for the same crime more than once after a verdict of acquittal or conviction. That way, the government can't just keep going after the same person in the hopes of finally getting them convicted.

Protection Against Multiple Punishments for the Same Offense: A person cannot be punished more than once for the same offence. This means that once a person has been sentenced, they cannot be given an additional sentence for the same crime.

However, keep the following in mind: The Separate Sovereigns Doctrine states that many tiers of government (such as the federal and state governments) have the authority to pursue prosecution for identical offences by their own legal systems. Someone may face murder charges in one court and civil rights charges in another, all stemming from the same incident.

Protection Against Retrial After Certain Mistrials: If a mistrial is declared due to a hung jury (the jury cannot reach a unanimous verdict), the prosecution can retry the case. However, if a mistrial is declared for reasons such as prosecutorial misconduct, a retrial may be barred.

With certain exceptions, the prosecution may be able to appeal some trial decisions (including the exclusion of evidence) without triggering double jeopardy, provided that the prisoner is not re-tried for the same crime.

The double jeopardy rule is only applicable in criminal proceedings and does not apply to civil disputes. As an example, consider the O.J. Simpson case, in which he was found guilty of wrongful death in a civil court, even though he was acquitted in the criminal trial. This means that a person's civil liability for damages associated with the same behaviour could still be challenged in a civil lawsuit.

All things considered, the double jeopardy clause is a cornerstone safeguard in the United States Constitution that serves to avoid judicial system abuse and guarantee justice is served fairly.

10. Bail

Bail is a series of pre-trial conditions put on a defendant to ensure that they will not obstruct the legal process. Court bail allows a prisoner to avoid jail time if they promise to appear in court when required. The posting of a bond, which can be money or property, with the court is often regarded in certain nations, especially the United States, as a means of releasing a suspect from pre-trial detention. The defendant's bail will be forfeited and they may be charged with failure to appear if they do not return to court. If the defendant shows up as instructed, their bail will be returned when the trial is over.

A suspect's bail conditions in some countries, such as the United Kingdom, may include the imposition of particular obligations for a set period. The granting of bail might occur either before or after the filing of charges in this situation. The posting of pre-charge or police bail allows for the freedom of a suspect while further investigation is underway.

Recognisance, which means "promise to appear in court without bail," or a summons to court without bail for lesser charges are two options available to defendants following arraignment. When a prisoner is considered to be avoiding court or the offence is particularly serious, the court may order their custody until trial, a practice known as remanding. The necessity of the suspect's appearance in court necessitates the granting of bail when imprisonment is not justified. The amount of bail is decided by various procedures, which might vary according on the degree and type of the accused's offence.

A cash or property deposit is the standard form of bail in the US. Bail in other nations is less extensive in terms of cash. Posting a sum of money, often called a bail bond or cash bail, allows the defendant to be released from pre-trial incarceration. The suspect will get their money back if they show up to all of their court dates.

It is possible to hire a bail bondsman to post bond for an accused person in 46 US states. In most parts of the world, this is considered criminal. If the court permits it when deciding to give monetary bail, bail bondsmen can be used legally in Germany. While money bail is rarely allowed in New Jersey and Alaska, it is illegal in Illinois, Kentucky, Oregon, and Wisconsin.

France

The French judge responsible for freedoms and custody or the examining magistrate can give bail before a trial begins, according to French law.

England

Acts, such as the Policing and Crime Act 2017, have made significant revisions to the major statutes governing bail in England, including the Bail Act of 1976 and the Police and Criminal Evidence Act of 1984.

The burden of proof is with the prosecution to show why bail should not be granted instead of custody, but this does not ensure that the defendant will get bail.

Bail can be granted in one of three ways in the English and Welsh legal systems:

Bail for the police. In exchange for not pressing charges, a suspect is freed with the condition that they report back to the station at the specified time.

Judgement of the court. A defendant must appear at their initial court hearing on the specified date and court after being granted bail following charges.

Release from jail. A suspect is released from custody following a court hearing to await additional investigation or the outcome of the case.

United States of America

"Excessive bail shall not be required" is the explicit wording of the 8th Amendment to the US Constitution, which guarantees the right to immunity from bond. A court has the discretion to deny bail if he or she believes it will not help bring the accused back to trial, and the judge decides what is considered "excessive" based on that discretion. While most states allow some kind of pre-trial release, the most prevalent is money bail, and the word "bail" is frequently used to refer to this type of deposit.

The suggested bond amount for a certain criminal offence is listed in a "bail schedule" that is available in many states. The judge has the discretion to establish bail during the arraignment, the initial court appearance, either at the amount shown on the schedule or at a different amount according to the particulars of the offence and the accused.

A suspect's chances of release are heavily influenced by their socioeconomic status. Racism is a prevalent grievance in the American bail system. Research has demonstrated that economically disadvantaged individuals are more likely to be subjected to jail conditions that illegally elicit guilty pleas, regardless of their actual or potential criminality. As a result, with a few exceptions, cash bail was eliminated in 2014 in both New Jersey and Alaska. Despite an effort by the California legislature to do away with cash bail in 2018, the measure was vetoed in November 2020 by California Proposition 25. On January 1, 2020, the bail reform legislation that New York enacted in 2019 became law, doing away with cash bail for numerous non-violent felony and misdemeanour cases. Prosecutors and law enforcement officers spearheaded public opposition to this statute, which ultimately led to its narrowing by the governor.

Judges take into account several considerations while setting bail, such as:

1. Bail amounts are usually determined by the seriousness of the offence.
2. There is a possibility that the defendant may try to evade justice by taking flight.
3. The age and health of the defendant.
4. A larger bail amount or even refusal of bail may be imposed based on a person's criminal record.

Strong ties to one's family, place of employment, and community can help reduce bail.

The defendant's bail may be rejected or set at a high amount based on public safety concerns.

Bail Types

Cash Bail: The full court-set bail amount is paid in cash by the defendant. In most cases, this sum is returned to the defendant upon their mandatory court appearances.

Surety Bonds: A surety bond is a type of bail bond wherein a bail bond agency agrees to post bail for a client in exchange for a non-refundable charge, usually between ten and fifteen per cent of the total bail amount. Collateral may be needed by the bail bond agency in order to guarantee the bond.

Release on Own Recognizance (ROR): The offender gets released from custody without posting bail if they agree to appear in court as scheduled. This type of release is called "Release on Own Recognisance" (ROR). People who are thought to pose little threat usually get this.

Property Bond: The bail sum is secured by the defendant or an agent pledging property, such as real estate, equal to the bail amount. The property can be confiscated if the offender does not show up for court.

Federal Bail: Conditions such as home confinement, electronic monitoring, or travel limitations may be imposed in lieu of or in addition to monetary bail in federal proceedings, as decided by federal law.

Bail Reform

A lot of people think the American bail system needs to be changed because:

People with lower incomes are disproportionately affected by the cash bail system, which causes them to be held in pretrial custody for longer periods of time, according to many.

Inequalities based on race, individuals of colour are disproportionately subject to greater bail amounts and a lower likelihood of being freed on their recognisance, according to many.

Problems with Public Safety: Those who are against the current system say it doesn't solve the problem of public safety as dangerous people with money can still get out.

The following reforms to the bail system have been passed by certain states:

Eliminating Cash Bail for Certain Offenses: For some low-level, non-violent offences, cash bail has been abolished by some states and municipalities.

Risk Assessment Tools: Bail judgements are guided by algorithms that evaluate the likelihood of reoffending or fleeing the country.

Pretrial Services: To make sure that defendants who are released pretrial show up for court and follow their release conditions, pretrial services offer monitoring and support.

In general, the bail system is still a controversial and ever-changing part of American law, even though it's supposed to strike a balance between the accused's rights and the necessity to guarantee their court appearance.

11. Appeal

An appeal is a formal procedure in which a party seeks a review by a higher authority of a decision that has already been made. The purpose of an appeal is twofold: first, to rectify a mistake; and second, to clarify and interpret the law.

The ability to appeal has been recognised in ancient Roman law since 509 BC in the Valerian and Porcian statutes. In later times, it made use of a convoluted system of appellate courts, with the emperor himself hearing certain cases.

The Appeal Process

Most litigants appeal lower court judgements and orders after the judgement already had taken place, while certain courts do allow appeals during the earlier phases of litigation. Appellate courts do not independently investigate facts, but they do examine issues of law de novo, from the beginning, which is a basic tenet of numerous legal systems. However, in most cases, unless there was an error in fact-finding, the appeal court will follow the trial court's record.

A lower court's or government agency's decision can be reviewed by the higher court through the certiorari process. A superior court in England might issue a writ of prerogative known as a certiorari to order the transfer of a lower court's record for review to a higher court.

The approval of a petition for review or certiorari by an appellate court typically initiates the appeal process. In contrast to trials, which are commonly conducted with juries in common law regimes, appeals are usually brought before a judge or panel of judges. Legal briefs, in which each side makes a lengthy written case, are typically submitted before oral argument. It is also possible for an amicus curiae to be granted permission by an appellate court to file a brief in favour of a certain party or stance. Once the parties have submitted their briefs, they may be given the chance to argue their case orally before a judge or panel of judges. It is common practice for judges to interrogate lawyers during oral arguments to test their reasoning or to promote their own legal views. Appellate courts settle the legal issues brought for review by issuing formal written conclusions after deliberating in chambers.

A reversal would mean that the lower court's decision was wrong; this would lead to the original judgement being annulled and the lower court being told to consider the matter again; an affirmation would mean that the lower court's decision was right.

Courts of appeal

While reviewing matters on appeal, appellate courts have the option to either uphold, overturn, or dismiss the lower court's ruling. Some courts serve a dual purpose, hearing cases of "first instance" as well as appeals. Higher appellate courts have the authority to examine decisions made by lower courts, including lower appellate courts, in countries where there is such a system. The Supreme Court or "court of last resort" is another name for a jurisdiction's highest appellate court in the USA, however, in some countries, the Appellate Court can be the highest, just below a Constitutional Court, as it is in South Africa.

The appeal process to a higher court.

Depending on the jurisdiction and the details of the case, there is a specific procedure to follow to appeal with a higher court. Nonetheless, these are the standard procedures followed in the US.

Establish Appeal Basis

The appeal must be supported by evidence.
Legal mistakes, such as giving the jury the wrong instructions or allowing the wrong evidence to be admitted or excluded.
Mistakes in procedure, poor evidence processing or judge or jury misconduct. Lack of proof to back the decision. Cases when the trial court abused its discretion.

Notice of Appeal

To appeal a trial court's decision, you must first notify the clerk of that court. Your intent to appeal is formally communicated to the court and the other party through this notice. It is required to be submitted within a particular time limit, typically thirty days following the judgement or decision that is being appealed.

Gather evidence for the record, for the appellate court.

Gather the necessary evidence from the trial court so that the appellate court can examine it.
Trial transcripts: All trial materials, including evidence and papers, as well as all court judgements and decisions.

Filing the Appellate Brief

Prepare an appellate brief and submit it to the appropriate court. Lay out the case and the law that supports the appeal. It should contain;

The facts and circumstances of the case.
A synopsis of the applicable statutes.
A case arguing that the trial court erred and that this impacted the result.   The conclusion should state the relief that is being sought, such as a fresh trial or a reversal of the judgment.

The Respondent Brief

In response, the opponent, known as the respondent, will submit a brief that will argue in favour of affirming the trial court's ruling.

Briefing the Respondent

In response, the other side, known as the respondent, will submit a brief that will argue in favour of affirming the trial court's ruling and that the trial court's decision should be upheld.

Reply Brief

For a response to the respondent's brief, you can submit a reply brief.

Reasoning with Oral Arguments

Oral arguments are scheduled by the appellate court in some instances. In these hearings, lawyers representing the parties involved present their positions and answer questions posed by the judges. Here is a chance to elaborate on things mentioned in the written briefings.

Ruling by the Court of Appeals

Significant judicial decisions, such as rulings by Courts of Appeal, provide multiple vital responsibilities in the legal system

Procedure for Reaching Decisions

The losing party (the appellant) has the right to submit an appeal following a lower court's ruling, claiming that the decision was influenced by legal mistakes.

Written briefs presenting the arguments of each side are submitted. The appellant's brief details the mistakes they believe were made, whereas the appellee's brief presents reasons to support the lower court's ruling.

Oral Arguments: When the court sees fit, it may set a date for the parties' lawyers to present their cases and field questions from the judges.

Before reaching a decision, the judges on the appeal examine the lower court's record, the parties' submissions, and any arguments presented orally. They discuss whether there were problems in the way the law was applied or in the procedures.

Written opinions—either a majority opinion, concurring opinions, or dissenting opinions—may be issued by the court. The court's official ruling is the majority opinion.

Decision Categories

The appellate court has reached a unanimous conclusion to affirm the lower court's ruling.

When an appeals court disagrees with a lower court's decision, it reverses the lower court's ruling.

The appellate court may order a new trial or other measures that are in line with its decision to be taken by returning the case to the lower court for additional procedures.

The appellate court has the discretion to partially modify the lower court's decision, rewriting some parts while maintaining others.

Decision-Related Consequences

Decisions made by the appellate court set the standard for how similar matters are to be decided in the future. Within the same jurisdiction, lower courts are obligated to adhere to these precedents.

These decisions aid in the development of the law by providing clarification and interpretation of statutes, regulations, and constitutional requirements.

Laws must be applied consistently across different cases and jurisdictions, and appellate courts do this by reviewing and ruling on decisions made by lower courts.

Justness and Fairness: Appellate review aids in making sure that trials are fair and that mistakes in the law that could result in unfair verdicts are fixed.

Additional Appeal

If you are dissatisfied with the outcome of your case at the appellate level, you have the option to take it to a higher appellate court, such as the Supreme Court of your state or the United States, for additional review. It is up to the higher court to decide whether to accept or reject the case, which usually involves submitting a petition for certiorari or some other type of discretionary review.

Important Issues to Think About

Due Dates and Deadlines: At every point in the appeal process, there is a tight timeframe. If a deadline is missed, the appeal may be dismissed.

Legal Representation: Due to the complexity of the process and the strictness of the procedural regulations, it is strongly recommended that you collaborate with an attorney with expertise in practising appeal law.

Financial Implications: You should be informed that there are expenses involved with submitting an appeal, such as the filing fee, the cost of preparing the transcript, and the cost of hiring an attorney.

It is vital to get legal assistance and research the regulations of the particular court handling the appeal because each jurisdiction may have specific procedures. This will ensure that you manage the process properly.

12. Conviction

A verdict finding an accused person guilty of a crime is known as a conviction in the legal system. The defendant may be found guilty after a judge or jury finds them guilty, after accepting a guilty plea, or after a trial by jury.

What we call a "not guilty" verdict is the inverse of a conviction. A "not proven" finding, which is equivalent to an acquittal in Scotland, is another possibility. The court can direct the defendant's acquittal even after a guilty verdict. Countries like New Zealand, Canada, Australia, and England use this, which is called a discharge.

Convictions of innocent individuals do occur within the framework of any criminal justice system. This problem might be partially alleviated by post-conviction remedy procedures and appeal systems. A "miscarriage of justice" occurs when a mistake results in an innocent person being convicted. The prosecution has the right to appeal acquittals in some legal systems but is forbidden to do so in others due to the concept of double jeopardy.

The court decides on a suitable punishment after a conviction has been handed down. Collateral effects of criminal accusations include not only the sentence but also other potential outcomes. A person's ability to travel to other nations, their ability to get a job, and their housing situation are all examples of areas that can be affected. An individual's criminal record is called their antecedents or "previous" in the UK and "priors" in the US and AU.

When a defendant is found guilty of the allegations against them in a criminal trial, it is known as a conviction in the legal system. The most important parts of a conviction are these:

Arrest and Charges: The first step in the procedure leading up to a conviction is an arrest made when there is probable reason to believe that an individual has committed a crime. Afterwards, the prosecutor submits the official accusations.

The defendant is officially accused and is allowed to enter a plea (guilty, not guilty, or no contest) during the arraignment.

Proceedings that take place before a trial begins: bail hearings, dismissal motions, plea negotiating, and more.

If the matter proceeds to trial, the trial can take place before a jury or before a judge alone. The prosecution must establish the defendant's guilt beyond a reasonable doubt.

Following the hearing of all sides' cases and arguments, the judge or jury will reach a decision. The jury in a criminal trial will typically vote "not guilty" or "guilty", though "not proven" is an additional option in Scotland, depending on the circumstances. Verdicts could vary between counts within the same case.

Different Kinds of Verdicts

Crimes that carry the weight of a felony include rape, murder, and armed robbery. Serious fines jail terms, or both, are common outcomes of felony convictions.

Petty stealing, simple assault, and vandalism are all examples of misdemeanour crimes. Sentences for misdemeanours are typically less severe and carry lighter fines, community service requirements, or prison terms.

A minor offence, such as a traffic violation, is considered an infraction. The usual punishment for infractions is a fine or other small penalty.

Special verdict

Instead of or in addition to finding guilt or responsibility, a jury in an English trial may reach a "special verdict" that focuses on particular facts.

Compromise verdict

Suppose some jurors give up their firm beliefs on one important issue in exchange for others giving up their settled views on another. In that case, the result is a compromise verdict, and the panel cannot accept it because it does not have unanimous approval.

General verdict

In a general verdict, the jury finds and concludes on all issues presented comprehensively. After reviewing the evidence and reaching a decision based on the facts, the jury follows the court's instructions and applies the law to reach a verdict, which concludes the case.

Directed verdict

The presiding judge of a jury trial has the authority to direct the jury to reach a specific judgment. After determining that a jury would be unable to reach a result in a different direction, the judge will often issue a directed verdict. The jury is relieved of their duty to reach a decision following a directed verdict. A judge may direct a verdict on all matters or just those that are specifically mentioned in the case.

Sealed verdict

If the judge, the parties, and the lawyers all need to return to court before the verdict can be announced, the judge may order the verdict to be sealed in an envelope. Once the court meets again, the judge receives the verdict, which is held in a sealed envelope.

Results from a Verdict

The court decides on punishment at a sentencing hearing after a conviction; the punishment is based on the gravity of the offence, the offender's prior criminal record, and other considerations. Prison time, community service, fines, or probation may be a part of a sentence.

A person's life can be negatively impacted by a conviction's impact on their criminal record. The sentencing process may include a period of probation or parole with certain requirements that a convicted individual must adhere to, either in place of or in conjunction with incarceration.

Post-Conviction Relief Appeal:

If the defendant believes that the trial judge made a mistake in deciding the case's conclusion, they can ask a higher court to review their conviction.

Claims of ineffective aid of counsel or requests for a new trial based on newly discovered evidence are examples of post-conviction motions.

A condemned individual can question the legitimacy of their arrest or incarceration through a Habeas Corpus action.

Clemency or Pardon: The individual serving their sentence has the option to petition the president or governor for clemency or pardon, which could result in a reduction or elimination of their term.

Removal of Records and Sealing of Files

The ability to seal or delete a conviction from public record means that it cannot be accessed without a court order in certain jurisdictions. This may help alleviate some of the lingering effects of a conviction.

The Effects of a Verdict, Conviction

The ability to vote, serve on a jury, and own weapons are all examples of civil rights that might be affected by a conviction.

Employment: People with criminal records may face reluctance from employers who run background checks.

Landlords have the right to reject tenants who have a record of specific crimes.

Regarding immigration, a conviction might lead to deportation or other immigration implications for non-citizens.

Because of the gravity of the situation, individuals concerned must give careful consideration to the judicial procedure and any post-conviction redress that may be available to them.

13. Acquittal

A defendant is formally and officially cleared of criminal charges when a court judgement declares them not guilty. It means that there was insufficient evidence to establish the defendant's guilt. Important components of acquittal include:

The Arrest and Charges: The proceedings leading up to an acquittal start with an arrest made based on probable cause that an individual has committed a crime. Subsequently, formal charges are filed by the prosecutor.

The arraignment is the formal accusation of a crime and the defendant's chance to enter a plea of guilty, not guilty, or no contest.

Pre-Trial Proceedings: Hearings on bail, discovery, motions filed before trial, and plea bargaining are all part of the pre-trial proceedings. Both the prosecution and the defence get their cases ready.

Trial: The trial could take place before a jury or a judge alone. Everybody gets a chance to lay forth their case and offer proof.

Verdict: Following the hearing of all sides' cases and arguments, the judge or jury will reach a decision. In cases when the prosecution is found not guilty by the jury or judge, the verdict is "not guilty," and the defendant is acquitted.

Kinds of Aquitals

Directed Acquittal: The judge may direct an acquittal in the absence of defence arguments if he or she finds that the prosecution has failed to provide enough evidence to warrant a conviction.

Jury Acquittal: When the jury considers all the evidence and decides that the defendant is not guilty, this is called a jury acquittal.

Bench Acquittal: When the judge concludes the defendant is not guilty based on his or her findings, this is called a bench acquittal.

Consequences of Acquittal

Immediate Release: If the defendant is currently in detention, they are usually released quickly after an acquittal.

Double Jeopardy Protection: The concept of double jeopardy prevents a defendant from facing a second trial for the same crime in the same jurisdiction.

Restoration of Rights: The right to vote, own weapons, and be free from job discrimination because of the charges is among the legal rights that an acquitted individual keeps or regains.

How an Acquittal Differs from a Dismissal

An acquittal occurs when the prosecution fails to prove the defendant's guilt with sufficient evidence. Then the defendant will be acquitted with a verdict of not guilty.

Dismissal: The prosecution decides to drop charges before or during the trial, usually because of problems with the trial process, insufficient evidence, or other legal considerations. Just because a case can't go forward doesn't mean the defendant is innocent.

Public Perception and Impact

Even if a defendant is found not guilty, they may still have to deal with the fallout of public opinion that goes along with it, which can lead to social shame and harm to their reputation.

Related civil actions might proceed even after a defendant is found not guilty in a criminal trial. Even after acquittal, a defendant may be subject to a civil suit for damages arising out of the same incident.

High Profile Acquittals

The public's view of the justice system can be influenced by high-profile acquittals. To name a few, there are:

In 1995, O.J. Simpson was found not guilty of the murders of Ronald Goldman and Nicole Brown Simpson.

George Zimmerman was found not guilty of killing Trayvon Martin in 2013.

Considerations of Law and Procedure

To avoid unjust convictions, the prosecution must establish guilt "beyond a reasonable doubt," an extremely high burden of proof.

In a trial by jury, the members of the jury decide whether the state has presented sufficient evidence to warrant a conviction.

It is essential for the legal system to have acquittals so that people are not unfairly punished when there is insufficient proof of their guilt.

14. Mandatory sentencing

Most crimes, especially those classified as serious or violent, carry mandatory sentence requirements, which stipulate that offenders must serve a particular amount of time behind bars. The legislature, not the judiciary, is responsible for producing these penalties, hence judges must adhere to the law. They are put in place to make sentencing go more quickly and to reduce the likelihood of unusual results caused by judges' discretion. Individuals found guilty of specific severe and/or violent offences are usually subject to mandatory sentencing, which entails a jail term.

The "moral vices" (drugs, alcohol, sex) and offences that endanger people's ability to make a living are frequently the targets of mandatory sentencing legislation. The basic premise is that perpetrators of certain crimes should not be reintegrated into society until they have been adequately punished. It is considered necessary to permanently remove offenders from society for certain crimes through a life sentence or, in extreme cases, the death penalty.

Under the system of mandatory sentencing, judges are obligated to hand down predefined, fixed punishments for particular offences, frequently without having the discretion to take into account the specifics of the case or the criminal. While this strategy has good intentions, to discourage criminal behaviour and standardise punishment, it might be perceived as unfair and cruel in some cases.

Aspects of Mandatory Sentencing

Important Elements of Mandatory Sentencing fixed penalties: Judges are severely limited in their ability to exercise discretion when it comes to sentencing since laws dictate particular minimum or fixed penalties for various offences.

Offences of a serious nature: Crimes involving drugs, violence, sex, and recurrence (e.g., "three strikes" statutes) sometimes result in mandatory penalties.

Goals: Making sentences consistent and fair, preventing dangerous offenders from reoffending, and reducing crime overall are the objectives.

Some Statutes Establishing Mandatory Sentences

The Laws of Three Strikes: Conviction for three felonies typically results in a life sentence under these statutes, which severely punish repeat offenders.

Possession or distribution of specific amounts of banned substances, as well as other drug-related offences, are subject to mandatory minimum terms.

The use of a firearm in a criminal offence carries stricter punishments.

Benefits of Sentencing Requirements

Lessens sentencing discrepancies by ensuring that comparable offences carry comparable penalties for consistency and uniformity.

Individuals may be discouraged from perpetrating criminal acts when they perceive the likelihood of facing harsh penalties.

Disablement: Eliminates dangerous criminals from society, which may lead to a decrease in crime rates.

Disadvantages of Sentencing Obligations

The inability of judges to take into account the specifics of each case raises concerns about the possibility of unduly severe punishments.

Jail overpopulation: Adds to the problem of jail overpopulation and drives up correctional system expenses.

Effects on Minorities: The judicial system's racial and socioeconomic inequalities are worsened when it disproportionately impacts minority groups.

Potentially leads to unfair results for those whose situations call for a more liberal approach, which is unfair in specific cases.

Legislative Changes:

There has been a growing movement to change or repeal mandatory sentencing laws, especially for non-violent drug offences. Drug courts, diversion programs, and restorative justice initiatives provide alternatives to jail for some criminals. Some jurisdictions have also established sentencing guidelines that give a range of punishments but leave room for some judicial discretion depending on the specifics of each case.

Conclusion

The decision of what charges to press against defendants can be shifted from judges to prosecutors under mandatory sentencing rules. Some people think mandatory sentences are a good way to be strong on crime, while others think they cause unfair outcomes and add to the problem of mass incarceration. The criminal justice system's treatment of mandatory punishment is still controversial. Its inflexibility has drawn complaints about its effect on justice, judicial discretion, and society, despite its stated goal of providing uniformity and deterrent. Lawmakers, campaigners, and legal experts are still trying to find a middle ground between people's rights, public safety, and justice by reforming these laws.

15. Suspended sentence

When a defendant is found guilty of a crime, the court may decide to wait for the execution of their sentence so that they might complete probation instead. This is called a suspended sentence. Most probation orders are considered satisfied when the offender does not violate the terms of their release and stays out of trouble with the law for the allotted time. The court has the authority to punish the defendant, along with any additional penalty for the new offence, if the offender commits another crime or violates the conditions of probation.

In a suspended sentence, the court finds the offender guilty but decides not to immediately impose a prison term; instead, the offender is placed on probation. The offender may be exempt from serving the initial sentence if they fulfil all terms imposed by the court throughout their probationary term.

Characteristics of a Suspended Judgement

When a defendant is found guilty or enters a plea of guilty, it is called a conviction.

Sentence Announcement: A sentence has been handed down by the court, but its execution has been put on hold.

While on probation, the defendant is required to adhere to certain guidelines.

Requirements: These may involve keeping a job, going to treatment or counselling programs, not using drugs or alcohol, avoiding more legal issues, and regular meetings with a probation officer.

The defendant may be eligible to have the suspended sentence reduced or revoked upon successful completion of the probationary term without infractions.

The court has the authority to revoke the suspension and reinstate the original sentence if the defendant violates the terms of probation.

Sentences That Have Been Suspended

Fully Suspended Sentence: The whole term is vacated, and the offender is released and sent free on probation.

Partially Suspended Sentence: The criminal serves some of the sentence before being placed on probation in a partially suspended sentence.

Suspended Sentences: Their Advantages

A second chance is a chance for rehabilitation rather than jail time.

Helps alleviate prison overcrowding by facilitating the release of non-violent criminals from prison.

Save Money: Reduces expenses related to jail.

Helps the ex-offender get back into society as a whole by letting them keep their jobs and keep in touch with relatives.

Problems with Suspended Sentences

Some probationed offenders run the risk of committing new crimes while out on parole.

Perception of Militancy: May be seen as a forgiving penalty, which could weaken the effectiveness of deterrence.

Difficulty with Supervision: Probation supervision that is both effective and efficient can be demanding on resources.

Probation Restrictions

Typical terms that may be imposed as part of a sentence that is suspended include:

Consistent check-ins with the probation officer.

Time restrictions

Drug and alcohol evaluations and rehabilitation.

Therapy or courses on controlling one's temper.

Prohibition of engaging in certain activities with specific persons.

Limitations on movement or permanent residence.

Violation of Probation

In the event of a probation violation, the court has the authority to:

Put an end to the defendant's sentencing suspension and have them complete their full term.

Add new requirements or lengthen the probationary period.

Reprimand with a warning or other form of intermediate punishment.

Determination of suspended sentence eligibility.

The following are examples of what may be required by law to receive a suspended sentence:

Smaller or less serious offences.

People who commit crimes for the first time or have a short criminal record.

Offenders who are determined to be rehabilitative through the process of probation.

Conclusion

Minor, non-violent offences and first-time offenders often receive suspended sentences in the United States. In deciding who is eligible and under what conditions, state legislation and judges' discretion are major factors.

In the United Kingdom, offenders convicted of less serious offences are often given suspended sentences with specified terms to adhere to, just like in the United States.

To find a middle ground between punishment and rehabilitation, a suspended sentence may be useful. By doing so, they can show that they are capable of complying with legal and societal standards while avoiding jail. To make sure it works as intended, which is to reduce recidivism and help with reintegration into society, it needs strict enforcement and monitoring.

16. Custodial sentence

This sentence cannot be imposed unless the court determines that the offence, or the combined offence with one or more related offences, was so severe that neither a fine nor a community sentence would be appropriate, according to the Criminal Justice Act 2003 of England and Wales. Minimum jail terms apply to certain serious offences, barring extraordinary circumstances. When the public's safety is in jeopardy, custodial punishments may be imposed.

A judicial judgment that punishes mandatory incarceration in a correctional facility, psychiatric ward, reformatory, or residential treatment program for substance abuse is known as a custodial sentence. A "custodial" sentence, as the name implies, calls for another entity to take responsibility for an individual and suspend their freedom.

Features of a Custodial Sentence Imprisonment:

The offender is required to serve a predetermined amount of time behind bars.

Deprivation of freedom: The main feature of a prison term is the taking away of the person's freedom.

The seriousness of the offence and the danger that the criminal poses determine the prison's security level, which might be minimum, medium, or highest.

Different Forms of Jail Time

Sentences of less than twelve months' duration are commonly imposed for infractions that are considered minor.

More serious offences have longer sentences (more than 12 months).

A life sentence means that the criminal must serve out their whole prison term behind bars. Parole may be an option once a specified amount of time has passed in certain jurisdictions for those serving life sentences.

With an indeterminate sentence, the parole board evaluates the offender's conduct and rehabilitation progress to establish an appropriate sentence length.

The Goal of Penal Penalties

The purpose of punishment is to make the criminal pay for their wrongdoing.

The purpose of deterrence is to dissuade repeat offenders and others from engaging in criminal behaviour.

To help a formerly incarcerated person become productive members of society again, rehabilitation programs offer classes, treatment, and opportunities to acquire new skills.

To safeguard the general populace against potentially harmful persons.

Factors Impacting Prison Terms

The length of a person's prison term is directly proportional to the seriousness of the offence.

A criminal record could result in heavier punishments for repeat offenders.

Remorse, collaboration with authorities, and the absence of prior offences are mitigating factors that might result in reduced sentences.

The use of violence, premeditation, or injury to susceptible victims are aggravating factors that can lead to heavier punishments.

The Situation in Correctional Institutions

Everyday Routine: Regular timetables for things like work, school, and play.

Recidivism Reduction Programs: Substance addiction treatment, job training, and educational opportunities are all part of the rehabilitation program.

Prisoners are expected to behave under the prison's norms and rules, and there will be repercussions for those who do not.

Under specific circumstances, prisoners may have the right to visitation rights.

Effects of Prison Terms

Loss of autonomy, estrangement from loved ones, and the possibility of good and bad behavioural shifts are all personal impacts.

The perpetrator's loved ones suffer the mental and financial toll of the crime.

Cost to society from running prisons and providing for convicts is known as the social impact.

Options Other Than Prison Time

When an offender is placed on probation, they are allowed to return to society under close supervision, but with specific limitations.

The criminal is required to serve the community by working unpaid for a certain amount of hours.

Fines are monetary penalties that are levied against the perpetrator.

Instead of a prison, the criminal is confined to their home under electronic monitoring as part of a house arrest.

The criminal may be able to avoid jail time under a suspended sentence provided they meet specific requirements.

Possible reform

Calls for reform and alternative sentencing have been heard in response to many jurisdictions' widespread problem of overcrowded jails.

The usefulness of prison sentences in rehabilitating criminals as opposed to just punishing them is a contentious topic.

Discussions about enhancing rehabilitation and assistance programs are prompted by the high recidivism rates among released inmates.

The heavy financial load on taxpayers and the exorbitant expense of prison maintenance.

Conclusion

The goals of the criminal justice system, which include punishment, deterrence, rehabilitation, and public safety, include the use of custodial sentences. Overcrowding, expenses, and finding the right balance between punishment and rehabilitation are some of the problems that these systems face, despite their effectiveness for specific crimes and offenders. One possible solution to these problems is to investigate and perhaps use alternatives to prison terms in appropriate instances.

17. Periodic detention

The criminal is free during the week but confined to prison on weekends (sometimes called "periodic detention" or "weekend detention") as part of a custodial sentence. Periodic detention, advocated for by those seeking to reform the penal system, was lauded for enabling incarcerated individuals to keep up with their jobs, keep in touch with loved ones, and avoid hanging out with more dangerous peers. The administration cost was likewise much lower.

Offenders serving sentences under periodic detention programs are permitted to do so at irregular intervals, such as on weekends or designated days, instead of serving their terms continually. By allowing criminals to keep their jobs, families, and community ties intact, this sentencing style seeks to strike a balance between punishment and rehabilitation.

Offenders serving sentences on intermittent bases may be required to report to prison on specific days or nights of the week.

Offenders are allowed to carry on with their usual lives, including their jobs or school, during the week.

Assists ex-offenders in keeping in touch with family and friends outside of prison, which lessens the negative effects of incarceration and speeds up the recovery process.

Periodic Detention Eligibility

Criteria for eligibility can differ by jurisdiction, but in general, they encompass:

Inmates Committed Non-Violent Offences: Usually designated for individuals who commit non-violent offences for the first time.

Offenders with solid work histories, strong educational commitments, or substantial family obligations are frequently considered seriously.

Based on the offender's circumstances and the nature of the offence, judges have the option to impose periodic detention.

Advantages of Retention Periods

Less Disruption: The offender's family life, work, and education are less likely to be negatively impacted.

Helps ex-offenders get back on their feet by letting them keep up good relationships and duties in the community.

Save Money: This alternative to full-time imprisonment lessens the financial strain on the penal system.

Possible reduction in recidivism rates through assisting ex-offenders in reentering society and sustaining stability.

Important Issues

Making sure that inmates follow the rules and adhere to the detention schedule may be a demanding ordeal that requires a lot of resources.

Offender Noncompliance: Offenders may not follow the schedule or commit additional offences during periods when they are not in detention.

Viewed by the public as a milder form of punishment, which could weaken the deterrence effect of the sentence.

Establishing Regular Detention

Orders from the Court: A sentencing order is issued by the court that details the conditions and timetable of periodic incarceration.

Places of Detention: Criminals are required to appear at certain correctional institutions, which could include regular prisons or specialised periodic detention centres.

Officers specialising in probation and parole oversee incarcerated individuals to make sure they follow the conditions of their release and help them get back on their feet.

Places implemented

As an alternative to life in prison, periodic detention has been implemented in several Australian states; however, it has since been phased out in other regions.

Although it has moved towards various community-based sentencing, New Zealand, like Australia, has used periodic detention.

United States of America: Periodic detention is used by certain U.S. jurisdictions, especially for low-risk offenders and minor offences, although it is not widely used.

Conclusion

Offenders can still attend to their families, jobs, and education while serving their sentence with periodic imprisonment, which strikes a good balance in sentencing. Recidivism can be reduced and the prison system can be relieved with its assistance in rehabilitation and reintegration into society. Ensuring compliance and addressing public impressions of leniency, however, needs good monitoring and administration.

18. Discharge sentence

When a court decides not to impose a typical punishment, such as jail time or a fine, following a conviction, this is called a discharge sentence. Rather, the criminal is either released conditionally or unconditionally by the court. Offenders convicted of lesser offences or for the first time typically receive sentences of this type.

Different Kinds of Discharge Penalties

Total Discharge:

No further action is taken and the offender is released without condition. Conviction is entered on the record, but no punishment is handed down.

Goal: This is a common strategy when the court decides that the mere act of being prosecuted and found guilty serves as a strong enough deterrent to warrant no further punishment.

Discharge with Conditions:

This means that the criminal is freed from prison under strict supervision for a predetermined amount of time.

Good behaviour, frequent meetings with the probation officer, or enrollment in specific programs (such as drug treatment or community service) are all examples of conditions that may be imposed.

The offender may face a more severe punishment if they are re-sentenced for the initial offence if they breach the terms.

Convictions are public records, but offenders can mitigate the severity of their sentences by fulfilling the terms of their release.

Factors of Discharge Eligibility

Used for less serious offences, sometimes referred to as minor offences.

Offender Status: Frequently used to describe people who have never had a criminal record.

Potential for Recovery: The court determines that the criminal has little risk of reoffending and has the potential to undergo rehabilitation without additional punishment.

Discharge Sentence's Advantages

Offender rehabilitation and reintegration into society are prioritised, allowing them to escape the detrimental effects of a prison sentence.

The long-term stigma of having a criminal record is lessened, especially in the instance of an absolute discharge, thanks to this.

Save Money: It helps save money by making less use of prisons and other types of punishment.

Judicial Flexibility: Gives judges more leeway to decide on a sentence that fits the crime and the offender's unique circumstances.

Problems and Rebuttals

The public may view the criminal justice system as being overly forgiving, which could reduce its effectiveness in deterring criminal behaviour.

Ensuring Adherence: It can be a resource-intensive process to ensure that offenders adhere to the terms of a conditional discharge.

Reoffending is a real possibility for some criminals, particularly if we fail to deal with the root causes of their criminal behaviour.

Illustrations and Authority Regions

In the United Kingdom, first-time offenders and those convicted of lesser offences often receive either an absolute or conditional discharge.

In Canada, as in the United Kingdom, small infractions are often punished with discharge sentences rather than harsher ones.

Discharge sentences are used in certain states and jurisdictions in the US, while their availability and usage might differ greatly.

Effects on offenders

However, the conviction remains on file and may have legal ramifications, such as impacting sentencing in the event of a subsequent offence, even though a discharge absolves the offender of immediate penalty.

Offender rehabilitation and prevention of recidivism are both aided by the availability of support services, such as counselling and drug treatment programs.

Jobs and Education: In contrast to a prison term, a discharge, especially an absolute discharge, might lessen the negative effects on educational and job prospects.

In summary,

Rehabilitation and reintegration, rather than the use of conventional punitive methods, are the primary goals of these sentences, which aim to address criminal behaviour. We must carefully assess their application to ensure they do not undermine the perceived effectiveness of the justice system, even while they offer major benefits including decreased costs and lesser repercussions on the offender's future.

19. Sentencing Rules and Guidelines

Based on the defendant's qualities and the nature of the criminal charge, sentencing guidelines establish a recommended sentencing range. Sentencing guidelines can be either optional or required for the specific crimes they address, depending on the jurisdiction.

In contrast, mandatory sentencing entails the establishment of statutory guidelines for criminal punishments, most commonly requiring minimum jail terms.

The purpose of sentencing guidelines is to provide judges with a framework within which to work when deciding on punishments for criminal convictions. With these rules in place, judges will be able to use their discretion based on the specifics of each case while also ensuring that the sentence is uniform, equitable, and proportional.

Goal of Sentencing Rules

Maintain sentencing uniformity by eliminating punishment discrepancies for comparable offences.

The seriousness of the crime should dictate the severity of the punishment.

Honesty: Outline the steps used to arrive at sentencing.

Judges should have considerable leeway to use their discretion because each case is different.

Sentencing Guidelines: Their Components

Offence Severity: The Guidelines classify many types of offences according to their severity, giving each a level or score.

Past Offences and Criminal History: Thinking about the defendant's criminal history, with points or categories representing the severity of their criminal behaviour in the past.

Possible Sentences: For any given offence and criminal record, determine a suitable punishment range, such as months or years in prison.

Causes and Effects, Both Negative and Positive: Provision for modifications in response to circumstances that either heighten (aggravate) or lessen (mitigate) the gravity of the punishment.

Rules tailored to certain situations, such as those involving drugs, violence, or white-collar fraud.

Application and Utilisation

State and Federal: Each level of government has its own set of regulations when it comes to sentencing; for example, in the United States, there are federal guidelines and state regulations.

The Judgement Panels and Sentencing Commissions: To keep the rules current and in line with current legal norms and societal values, they are generally developed and maintained by independent agencies or commissions.

Judicial Training for Judges: Judges get instructions on how to use the guidelines while deciding on sentencing.

Benefits of Guideline Sentencing

Consistent sentencing: This gives defendants, solicitors, and the general public a sense of security.

Helps bring about a lessening of unfair sentencing discrepancies for comparable offences.

Transparency: Enables the examination and appeal of sentence judgements made by judges.

Efficient Judicial procedure: Establishes a transparent framework that expedites the sentencing procedure.

Disadvantages of Sentencing Guidelines

Judges may have less leeway to adjust sentencing based on the specifics of each case as a result of less judicial discretion.

Sentencing guidelines that fail to consider individual circumstances run the risk of being either severe or too light.

Inconsistent application may result from the rules' complexity and difficulty of navigation.

Systems that Use Sentencing Guidelines

Sentencing Guidelines of the United States (USSG): Sentencing ranges are determined using a grid system that considers the gravity of the offence and the offender's past record; these guidelines were created for federal crimes.

The United Kingdom Sentencing Council offers ranges and considerations for different offences as well as guidelines for judges in England and Wales.

In Australia, the Sentencing Advisory Council in Victoria is one of several state-level bodies that provide recommendations on fair sentencing procedures.

Contributing and Reducing Elements

The use of a weapon, previous convictions, or the commission of the offence in the presence of children are all examples of aggravating factors that might lead to a harsher punishment.

Considerations that can lessen the harshness of the punishment include the offender's age, absence of a criminal record, expressions of regret, and cooperation with law enforcement.

Variations from the Guidelines for Sentencing

Judges have the discretion to impose a sentence that is either more severe or less severe than the guidelines call for when considering individual cases.

Justification: A written explanation defending a judge's decision to depart from the rules is usually required.

Higher courts have the authority to evaluate and, if necessary, appeal sentences that do not adhere to the criteria.

Conclusion

To ensure that sentencing choices are fair, consistent, and transparent, the criminal justice system relies on sentencing guidelines. Although they offer a framework for judges to follow, they also leave room for the discretion that is needed to consider specific case conditions. A key problem in implementing guidelines is finding a balance between their rigidity and the requirement for individualised justice.

20. Guilt in Criminal Law

In criminal law, actus reus, meaning a guilty act, is an element of a crime. Mens rea, meaning guilty mind, is also needed. To be legally responsible for a crime is what the term "guilt" means in criminal law. Judgement is the conclusion reached by a court or jury regarding the defendant's legal responsibility for the offence against which they are charged. A number of essential elements come together to form the notion of guilt, which is at the heart of criminal procedures.

Criterion for Criminal Guilt (Actus Reus, "Guilty Act"):

Committing the offence physically or failing to act when legally obligated to do so, is a guilty act.

Some examples include stealing (theft), attacking (battery), and tax evasion (not filing taxes).

The Guilty Mind (Mens Rea):

The frame of mind that criminals use when planning their crimes. There are varying degrees of intentionality required for many crimes, including carelessness, recklessness, knowledge, and purpose. As an illustration, consider the following crimes: manslaughter, drug possession, and intent to kill.

Causation:

For an offence to be committed, the defendant's acts must lead to the specified harm or consequence.

The "but for" test pertains to factual causation, while the proximate cause is used in legal contexts.

Concurrence:

A person must be in the right mental state and the actus reus must happen at the same time. In order for an offence to be committed, the defendant must have been guilty in mind when it was done.

Absences of Defenses:

The prosecution has the burden of proving that the defendant has no legitimate legal defences (such as insanity, self-defence, or duress) that could clear their name and exonerate them.

Trial Procedure for Establishing Guilt:

This burden of proof rests squarely on the shoulders of the prosecution, who must establish guilt "beyond a reasonable doubt."

The defence has the opportunity to introduce arguments and evidence in an effort to cast doubt on the prosecution's case or show that they have failed to meet their burden of proof.

Judge or jury: At a jury trial, members of the jury deliberate and reach a verdict on the defendant's guilt or innocence.

On a bench trial, the judge decides whether or not the defendant is guilty.

Verdict:

Guilty: The defendant is guilty of the offence as alleged.

Not Guilty: When a defendant receives an acquittal, it indicates that the prosecution was unable to establish guilt beyond a reasonable doubt.

A retrial may be necessary if the jury is unable to reach a unanimous verdict, a situation known as a hanging jury.

The Presumptions and Legal Standards

It is presumed that the accused is innocent.

It is believed that a defendant is innocent until proven guilty. The onus of proof is on the prosecution.

Valid Doubt: For a criminal trial, the burden of proof is on the prosecution to provide sufficient evidence to reach a conviction. The prosecution has the burden of proving the defendant's guilt beyond a reasonable doubt for the judge and jury.

Factors Affecting the Evidence of Guilt:

Types include forensic evidence, circumstantial evidence, witness testimony, and tangible evidence.

Admissibility: The evidence must be pertinent to the case and legally collected.

Mens rea and intent:

Levels of Intent: The degree of intent required for a certain offence varies, which influences the verdict of guilt. For instance, manslaughter may merely require recklessness, but first-degree murder may require premeditation.

Defences:

Common defences include alibi, error of fact, duress, insanity, and self-defence. A successful defence may result in a reduced charge or an acquittal.

Post-conviction Relief Appeals and Appeals:

Reasons: Inadequate evidence, erroneous trial procedures, or misapplied legislation.

Result: The conviction may be upheld, or overturned, or the matter may be remanded for a fresh trial by the appellate court.

Relief After Conviction:

Techniques: Motions for a fresh trial, habeas corpus petitions, and pleas for reduced sentences.

Goal: To discuss fresh evidence or possible miscarriages of justice.

Conclusion

In criminal law, guilt is a multifaceted and intricate concept that involves the interaction of several factors, including causation, mens rea, actus reus, and the lack of defences. Guilt is decided properly and justly thanks to the judicial procedure, legal requirements, and ideas like the presumption of innocence and proof beyond a reasonable doubt. To ensure that justice is done and to navigate the criminal justice system, it is essential to comprehend these elements.

21. Totality Principle

Judgement based on the totality concept seeks to ensure that a person's whole criminal conduct is fairly and appropriately reflected in their sentence, without being unduly severe or lenient, when sentencing for many offences is considered. By taking the offender's actions into account holistically, this approach guarantees that the overall penalty is commensurate with the gravity of the offences committed.

Totality Principle Elements

Equal distribution:

The entire sentence must be fair and proportional to the seriousness of the offence, striking a balance between harshness and leniency.

Cutting Down on Lengthy Sentences:

The court's goal is to prevent a sentence that would be unduly lengthy or punitive if the punishments for each offence were simply added together.

Making Punishment Appropriate:

Punishment ought to be commensurate with the gravity of the crimes committed, and the entire sentencing ought to reflect that.

Implementation of the Totality Principle in Sentences:

When sentencing numerous offences, the courts determine whether the terms should run concurrently or consecutively.

The totality principle is used by the court to make sure that consecutive punishments are proportional.

Putting Sentences Together:

When sentencing a person for repeated offences, the court takes the cumulative effect of those offences into account.

If a person is found guilty of three different offences, the court may decide to lower the total sentence rather than just adding the penalties for each one. This is done to prevent the punishment from being too harsh.

Judgement:

When deciding how to apply the totality concept, judges take into account a variety of variables, including the seriousness of the crimes, the offender's background, and the need of rehabilitation and deterrence.

The Totality Principle Takes Offence Seriousness and Type into Account:

The gravity of each crime, its characteristics, and any extenuating or mitigating factors.

Background of the Offender:

An offender's age, health, criminal record, and rehabilitation prospects are all factors in their unique personal situation.

Victim Impact:

The pain endured by victims and the importance of bringing them closure and justice.

The Common Good:

It is important to make sure that punishment is effective in discouraging similar behaviour and to keep public faith in the justice system.

Jurisdictions and UK:

Judges are encouraged to consider the complete crime when determining a sentence, as the Sentencing Council guidelines stress the totality principle.

The guideline states that judges should make sure the total sentence is long enough to reflect the gravity of the offences without being excessively harsh.

American territory:

Although the totality principle is not specifically included in the United States federal sentencing guidelines, judges frequently use similar reasoning to ensure that penalties for multiple offences are fair and equitable.

When deciding whether sentences should run consecutively or concurrently, the notion is intrinsic.

Prior decisions and case law

Case law: Higher courts often offer direction on how to balance penalties for several offences, and it frequently highlights the application of the totality principle.

Rules set by the courts: Ensure sentencing methods are consistent and fair by influencing how subordinate courts implement the principle.

Conclusion

Just, fair, and proportional sentencing for many offences are guaranteed by the totality principle. Courts strive to give sentences that fairly represent the gravity of the criminal behaviour without being too harsh by taking into account the cumulative effect of the offences and the offender's general conduct. In order to keep the public's faith in the justice system intact, this approach strikes a balance between punishment, deterrence, and rehabilitation.

22. Dangerous offender

A "dangerous offender" is someone who has committed multiple violent or sexual offences in the past and is considered to be a major threat to society because of this. In order to safeguard the public, this classification permits harsher and frequently indeterminate sentencing. Determining whether an individual is a dangerous offender requires a comprehensive evaluation of their past actions and circumstances, while the specifics of this process could differ from one jurisdiction to another.

Classification of Dangerous Offenders

Determination Requirements:

Behaviour Pattern: A record of major sexual or violent offences.

There is strong evidence that this individual is likely to commit other violent or sexual offences in the future.

Crimes of a Serious Nature: These crimes are usually very destructive or egregious.

Procedure within the Law:

The dangerous offender classification is typically requested by the prosecution following a significant conviction.

A psychiatric or psychological evaluation of the offender's reoffending risk may be ordered by the court.

At a judicial hearing, witnesses and evidence, including opinions from experts on the crime's risk to society, are presented.

Indeterminate Sentences:

Criminals may be ordered to serve an indefinite amount of time in prison, with parole eligibility being reviewed at regular intervals.

For the sake of public safety, dangerous offenders are typically subject to enhanced surveillance upon parole.

The major objective of preventive detention is to render the offender unable to commit more crimes for the duration that they continue to constitute a threat.

Examples of Jurisdiction

Canada:

Provisions Regarding Dangerous Offenders: Offenders who have committed major offences involving bodily harm and are considered to have a high likelihood of committing further offences can be labelled as dangerous under the Canadian Criminal Code.

Indeterminate terms: Offenders deemed dangerous can be given indeterminate terms, with the Parole Board of Canada reviewing their release eligibility every two years.

United States of America:

Habitual Offender Laws: "Three strikes" legislation allows for the mandatory life sentence without the possibility of release for those convicted of several major felonies in some states.

Laws Regarding Sexually Violent Predators (SVPs): After serving their prison terms, several jurisdictions' residents who are considered SVPs can be civilly committed.

England and Wales:

In the United Kingdom, offenders deemed dangerous are subject to provisions in the Criminal Justice Act of 2003 that permit lengthy prison terms and indefinite incarceration.

Indeterminate jail terms known as "public protection" (IPP) are handed down to criminals who constitute a substantial threat to the general population.

Analysed and Potential Risks

Assessments in Mental Health and Psychology:

Evaluations centre on the criminal's emotional well-being, character attributes, criminal history, and chances of recovery.

Reoffending risk assessment tools include the Static-99 and the Hare Psychopathy Checklist.

Important Matters To Take Into Account:

Offence Type: How often and how serious the offences were in the past.

Behaviour Patterns: Signs of ongoing hostile or predatory conduct.

Mental health disorders: a list of diagnoses that might increase the risk of sexual or violent crime.

Remarks

Civil Liberties:

There are legitimate worries regarding the possibility of civil liberties and human rights breaches associated with the endless nature of punishments for dangerous offenders.

Many feel that these labels lead to overly harsh punishments that aren't really warranted.

Efficiency and Recovery:

If dangerous offenders have access to sufficient rehabilitation programs and if indefinite incarceration is beneficial in avoiding recidivism are topics of dispute.

Some people think that punishment isn't the best approach, and that greater focus should be on treatment and rehabilitation.

Inequalities and Harassment:

Possible racial, socioeconomic, or mental health biases in the application of dangerous offender classifications are among the issues that have prompted concerns.

Conclusion

People with a history of major offences and a high probability of reoffending are managed using the dangerous offender classification, a legal tool. Questions concerning civil freedoms, the balance of punishment and rehabilitation, and the possibility of inequities in its administration arise alongside the program's stated goal of protecting society by incapacitating high-risk persons. To guarantee a fair and appropriate use of the designation, courts must thoroughly evaluate each case.

23. Capital punishment

Execution by the state as a form of criminal punishment is a legal procedure that goes by several names, including capital punishment and the death sentence. "Capital offences" is the common term for crimes that carry the death penalty. The main features of the death penalty are as follows:

Crucial Elements of the Death Penalty Crimes Capable of Execution:

Murder is the most prevalent capital offence, and it is often more severe when there are numerous victims, the crime is extremely horrible, or a law enforcement officer is killed.

When people commit acts with the intent to sow chaos and bloodshed, we call it terrorism.

The death penalty is a punishment for narcotics trafficking in certain nations.

Murder: Murder, particularly when it involves children, carries the death penalty in some countries.

Violations of state sovereignty or security, such as espionage and treason, are crimes.

Procedure within the Law:

Prior to sentencing, the defendant is subject to a trial in which his or her guilt is required to be established beyond a reasonable doubt. In the event of a conviction, the appropriateness of the death penalty is decided upon in a distinct sentencing phase.

Review and Appeals: A thorough appeals procedure to prevent unjust executions and guarantee a fair sentencing. This may need a trip to the highest court in the land, whether it's a federal or state court in the United States.

Pardoning or commuting a death sentence to life in prison is an example of clemency. The executive branch includes the president and governor, who have the power to do this.

Procedures for Carrying Out:

Injection of a lethal dose of medicines to cause coma, paralysis, and death is the most prevalent procedure in the United States.

The convicted person is subjected to a lethal electric shock in the process of electrocution.

The condemned are shot by a group of executioners at the same time in a firing squad.

The condemned person is hung from a high place as a noose is put around their neck.

Decapitation by sword or guillotine, a practice practised in certain nations, is known as beheading.

Justifications for and against the death penalty

Proponents of capital punishment contend that it discourages heinous acts by creating a sense of dread of harsh retribution.

The concept of retribution refers to the practice of exacting proper punishment for particularly egregious wrongdoing.

Ensuring that dangerous criminals are unable to re-offend is crucial to public safety.

Brings Victims' Families a feeling of Finality: Gives them a feeling of finality and justice.

Opposing Views:

The possibility of carrying out the death penalty on innocent individuals as a result of court mistakes, faulty evidence, or misconduct leads to the risk of wrongful convictions.

It is regarded as cruel, demeaning, and a breach of human rights, including the right to life.

The expense of maintaining death row facilities, as well as the time and money spent on trials and appeals, drives up the cost of capital prosecutions.

Abolitionist Nations: A Global Perspective

For reasons related to human rights, a few nations have done away with capital punishment altogether.

This includes every country in the European Union, Australia Canada, and the majority of countries in Latin America.

Countries with the death penalty is still in use:

The death penalty is still in use in some nations for reasons related to religion, culture, or national security.

Countries like Iran, Saudi Arabia, China, and India are examples.

Shifts and Currents:

The United Nations and other international organisations are calling for an end to the death penalty, and there is a growing movement to abolish or at least temporarily halt executions around the world.

More stringent protections against wrongful execution have been put in place by some nations, while others have narrowed the scope of capital offences.

Issues of Law and Ethics

Treaties and International Law:

The death penalty is an issue that has been the subject of numerous international treaties and conventions, including the ICCPR, which seeks to limit and control its application.

The ICCPR's Optional Protocols demand an end to capital punishment.

Conflicts on Morality:

Many people have strong opinions on the subject, including whether or not it is moral to kill someone as a punishment, whether or not it can be applied discriminatorily, and what happens if innocent people are executed.

Life without the possibility of release is a more compassionate and successful option, according to some.

Issues of Law and Ethics

Treaties and International Law:

The death penalty is an issue that has been the subject of numerous international treaties and conventions, including the ICCPR (International Covenant on Civil and

Political Rights), which seeks to limit and control its application.

The ICCPR's Optional Protocols demand an end to capital punishment.

Conflicts on Morality:

Many people have strong opinions on the subject, including whether or not it is moral to kill someone as a punishment, whether or not it can be applied discriminatorily, and what happens if innocent people are executed.

Life without the possibility of release is a more compassionate and successful option, according to some.

24. Execution warrant

A court or an authorised government official, like a governor, can issue an execution warrant to authorise the execution of a person with a death sentence. The necessary authorities are authorised to carry out the death sentence by the warrant, which stipulates the time, place, and method of execution. The most important parts of an execution warrant are as follows:

Importance of Execution Warrants:

Warrants are usually issued by higher courts, authorised executive officials, or the trial judge who presided over the case.

Timeline: It is released once the sentence has been upheld and all avenues of appeal and post-conviction remedies have been explored.

What the Warrant Covers:

The name and case number of the sentenced person are included in the warrant.

The details of the crime that resulted in the death penalty are outlined in it.

Date, time, place, and manner of execution (such as fatal injection or electrocution) are detailed in the execution details.

Signature Authorization: Signed by the issuing authority, such as the judge or governor.

Execution of the Order:

Officials at the jail or execution site, as well as the condemned person's legal representative, are informed when a warrant is issued.

Logistics and the execution protocol are finalised as part of the preparations made by the authorities at the execution facility.

Considerations of a Legal and Procedural Nature:

The execution must adhere to all applicable laws and procedures, including any applicable federal or state rules, and the warrant guarantees this.

When further evidence or legal concerns emerge, the execution can be temporarily halted through legal interventions like stays of execution.

Conviction and the Sentencing Process that Results in an Execution Warrant:

A trial court finds the defendant guilty of a deadly crime and hands down the death penalty.

Grievances and Relief Following Conviction:

Multiple appeals and post-conviction hearings check the legitimacy and justice of the conviction and sentence.

The Supreme Court is one possible destination for appeals after navigating federal appellate courts and state courts.

Review in Final:

If the death penalty is affirmed after all appeals and other legal avenues have been explored, the matter will be returned back to the trial court or appropriate authorities for a final decision.

Warrant Issuance:

The execution warrant is issued by the authorised authority, who also sets the execution date and hour.

Moral Considerations and Ethical and Legal Disputes:

There are moral concerns regarding the state's involvement in the taking of a life that are brought up by the issuance of execution warrants.

Those who are against the death penalty point to the possibility of wrongful executions and call for more humane forms of punishment.

Legal Obstacles:

New evidence, changes in public opinion, or procedural mistakes are all possible reasons to contest an execution warrant.

Common legal options to postpone or reduce the death penalty include pleas for clemency and stays of execution.

Conclusion

The last formality in the procedure of capital punishment is a vital legal document known as an execution warrant. It represents the last step in a protracted legal procedure that sought to guarantee the legitimacy and fairness of the death penalty. In spite of its importance from a legal standpoint, the issuance of an execution warrant remains at the centre of discussions over the ethical, legal, and human rights consequences of the death penalty.

25. Cruel and unusual punishment

An inhumane, unduly severe, or disproportionately large sentence is deemed to be "cruel and unusual punishment" according to legal standards. The Eighth Amendment, which forbids such punishments, is most commonly linked with this idea. A number of international human rights treaties and the legal systems of numerous other nations also reflect the notion.

Cruel and unusual punishment, as defined by law, primarily involves:

The Eighth Amendment to the United States Constitution states that no one shall be subject to harsh and unusual punishments, exorbitant fines, or excessive bail.

Treaties and International Law: Cruel, inhuman, or humiliating treatment or punishment is prohibited by various treaties, including the United Nations Convention Against Torture.

Interpretation by the Judiciary:

Courts determine what constitutes cruel and unusual punishment in light of changing social norms and standards of decency.

Decisions in Court: Roper v. Simmons (2005), Gregg v. Georgia (1976), and Furman v. Georgia (1972) are noteworthy cases that have influenced how this principle is understood and used in the United States.

Arguments concerning Cruel and Unusual Punishment

The severity of the penalty should reflect the gravity of the offence. Cruel and unusual punishments include disproportionate sentencing, such as lengthy jail terms for very little crimes.

Dignity for Humans:

Cruel and unusual punishments are those that dishonour human dignity or cause needless bodily or mental suffering.

Procedures for Carrying Out:

Certain types of execution, which involve needless pain, can be contested as cruel and unusual. As an example, there are valid ethical and legal issues about fatal injection mistakes.

Confinement Restrictions:

Overcrowding, inadequate medical treatment, and extended periods of solitary confinement are all examples of inhumane prison circumstances that could be considered cruel and unusual punishment.

Notable Cases Decided by the United States Supreme Court:

A de facto moratorium on capital punishment was instituted after the Supreme Court's ruling that the inconsistent and arbitrary use of the death penalty constituted cruel and unusual punishment.

In the case of Gregg v. Georgia (1976):

The death penalty, with additional standards to guarantee its equitable and uniform implementation, was reinstated when the Court upheld amended state statutes imposing the death penalty.

The decision in the case of Roper v. Simmons:

In light of changing moral standards, the Supreme Court declared that it is unlawful to execute juvenile offenders.

Virginia v. Atkins (2002):

Executing people who have an intellectual disability is deemed unconstitutional by the Court.

Human Rights Convention of the European Union (ECHR):

Torture and other cruel, humiliating, or degrading forms of punishment are outright forbidden under Article 3. An interpretation and application of this criteria is made by the European Court of Human Rights.

Consensus Against Torture within the UN:

Outlaws the use of torture and other cruel, inhumane, or degrading forms of punishment or treatment. It is the responsibility of each member state to ensure that their own territory is safe from such threats.

The ICCPR guarantees citizens' civil and political rights including:

Torture and other cruel, inhuman, or humiliating treatments or punishments are forbidden by Article 7.

The Death Penalty: A Contentious Issue

The question of whether capital punishment constitutes cruel and unusual punishment is an ongoing one, with many voicing worries regarding execution techniques and the possibility of false convictions.

Parole-Free Life (LWOP):

Life sentences without the chance of release are very contentious, particularly when applied to minor offenders. Some think LWOP is too severe and doesn't take rehabilitation into account enough.

Isolation as a Prisoner:

Because of the profound psychological impact it has, prolonged solitary confinement is being looked down upon as strange and cruel.

Conditions in Prison:

Major issues under the cruel and unusual punishment standard include inhumane jail circumstances, such as inadequate healthcare, overcrowding, and abuse.

Conclusion

To guarantee humane treatment within the legal system, it is essential to outlaw cruel and unusual punishment. Maintaining order, administering justice, and defending human dignity are constantly being balanced, and this is shown in how its interpretation and implementation change over time in response to societal norms and judicial precedents. Legal standards and arguments on punishment techniques around the world are still influenced by the principle.

26. Imprisonment

Confining those guilty of crimes in a controlled environment serves as both a punishment and a means of society's protection. Deterrence, retribution, rehabilitation, and incapacitation are some of its many functions. Penalties and sentencing guidelines differ greatly from one jurisdiction to another, from one seriousness of crime to another, and from one offender's situation to another.

Crucial Facets of Detention

Forms of Solitary Confinement:

The length of a jail sentence might vary from a few days to the rest of a person's life without the possibility of release.

Individuals who are determined to pose a threat to the community or who are believed to be a flight risk may be detained in custody prior to their trial.

For criminals under the age of eighteen, there are specialised institutions and programs known as juvenile detention centres.

Female inmates, those serving in the military, and those with mental health issues are just a few examples of the groups served by specialised prisons.

Goals of incarceration:

Retribution refers to the act of punishing the perpetrator for their deeds.

Dissuading the criminal and others from engaging in criminal behaviour is the goal of deterrence.

Rehabilitation entails facilitating convicts' readjustment to society through various programs.

Taking someone out of the community who poses a threat to public safety is an incapacitating measure.

Prison Environment:

A person's living conditions encompass their housing, nutrition, healthcare, and opportunities for physical activity.

Inmates still have some rights, including the right to a fair trial, the ability to retain an attorney, and safety from torture and other cruel and unusual punishments.

Educational and vocational programs, therapy for substance misuse, and counselling are all components of rehabilitation programs.

Protections under the Law and in Procedure:

Ensuring that incarceration follows a just and lawful trial is the essence of due process.

The right to appeal one's conviction or incarceration conditions is a fundamental component of due process for all inmates.

The systems of parole and probation provide for supervised conditional release.

Moral Principles and Global Human Rights

The Nelson Mandela Rules are a set of universally accepted minimum standards for the treatment of inmates.

Inmates' health, dignity, and rehabilitation should be the primary concerns in the establishment of all prison policies and procedures.

Prison Regulations in Europe:

Give the Council of Europe member states certain rules to follow when it comes to prison management and humane treatment of inmates.

The ICCPR guarantees citizens' civil and political rights including:

Humanity and respect for the inherent dignity of every person deprived of their liberty are guaranteed under Article 10.

Prison Overcrowding: A Review of the Problems and Challenges

Inadequate housing, higher rates of violence, and limited resources are all results of jail overpopulation.

Issues related to mental health:

Effective mental health care and assistance are necessary because of the high prevalence of mental illness among incarcerated individuals.

The phenomena of recidivism:

Effective rehabilitation and reintegration programs are necessary to break the cycle of recidivism and incarceration.

Selling off assets:

Concerns about affordability, healthcare quality, and the morality of for-profit prisons have arisen in response to the proliferation of private prisons.

Inequality and Discrimination:

There is still a serious problem with racial and socioeconomic disparities in sentencing and jail conditions.

Important Features Organised by US Jurisdiction:

The incarceration rate in the United States is among the highest globally.

Federal, state, and private jails all make up the criminal justice system.

The use of solitary confinement, overcrowding, and high recidivism rates are important issues.

The Scandinavian Style:

Prisons in Norway, for example, are constructed to look like regular houses so inmates may focus on rehabilitation and reintegration.

Providing substantial support for education and job training and treating inmates with dignity are priorities.

China:

Forced labour and other inhumane practices are hallmarks of the jail system.

Dissidents and political prisoners frequently endure especially harsh treatment.

England and Wales:

Many have voiced their disapproval of the overcrowding, violence, and lack of mental health services within the United Kingdom's jail system.

The goal of the recent revisions is to lower the recidivism rate and enhance rehabilitation programs.

In conclusion

The criminal justice system's use of imprisonment strikes a delicate balance between the objectives of public safety, rehabilitation, deterrence, and punishment. Although incarceration is an effective means of reducing crime, it is essential that nations find new ways to manage and treat their incarcerated populations to address persistent problems with overcrowding, mental health, recidivism, and human rights violations.

27. Life imprisonment

A person is sentenced to spend the rest of their life in jail as a kind of punishment known as life imprisonment. Murder, terrorism, and other heinous acts typically carry this punishment. Life sentences, along with their characteristics, such as whether or not parole is possible and under what conditions, differ from one jurisdiction to the next.

Crucial Elements of Life Imprisonment

Different Forms of Life Sentence:

The offender is expected to spend the remainder of their life behind bars and is not eligible for parole, which is known as life without parole (LWOP).

Life on Parole: Depending on the jurisdiction and the type of the offence, the individual may become parole-eligible after serving a certain number of years.

Considerations of a Legal and Procedural Nature:

Considerations such as the gravity of the crime, the offender's criminal record, and the specifics of the case are considered throughout the sentencing process, which may result in a life sentence for the most heinous of offences.

Anyone with a life sentence has the legal right to seek a judicial review of their conviction and sentence.

Prisoners who may be eligible for parole must appear before a parole board regularly for evaluations of their release eligibility.

Life Imprisonment's Goal:

Functioning as a penalty commensurate with the seriousness of the offence: this is retribution.

A deterrent is something that makes others think twice before committing a crime of a similar kind.

Incapacitation: Keeping potentially harmful people out of society.

Providing possibilities for rehabilitation in some circumstances with the intention of ultimate reintegration into society is known as rehabilitation.

Views from Other Countries on the American Scene:

Proliferation: In both federal and state courts, life sentences with or without parole are frequently imposed.

Cases sparking controversy: The usage of life sentences for adolescents and non-violent criminals has sparked discussions in the United States.

Issues like mandatory minimum sentences and the application of life without parole for specific crimes are the focus of continuing efforts to reform sentencing practices.

Continental Europe:

Human Rights: The European Convention on Human Rights had an impact on several European nations, leading them to emphasize rehabilitation and compassionate treatment.

When thinking about parole, it's important to keep in mind that many European countries have structures that make it possible, which shows that they value the chance for rehabilitation.

Scandinavia:

Norway is one of few countries that places a strong emphasis on rehabilitation as a means of sentencing, with parole options built into the system and life sentences being extremely unusual.

Humane Conditions: Inmates are encouraged to rehabilitate and maintain their dignity in prison settings that are designed to mimic everyday existence.

Various Other Courts:

Legal traditions, cultural beliefs, and crime rates all play a role in shaping how other nations handle life sentences.

Concerns about human rights: life sentences have come under fire in several nations for being too severe or cruel.

Disagreements and Discussions

Dignity and Human Rights:

The right to hope and the opportunity for rehabilitation and reintegration are allegedly violated by a life sentence without parole, according to critics.

Conditions of Confinement: Issues about the compassionate treatment of lifers in prison, including their availability of medical treatment, psychological support, and chances to participate in meaningful pursuits.

Individuals Under the Age of 18:

U.S. Supreme Court Decisions: A growing knowledge of juvenile growth and guilt has led to findings that mandatory life without parole for juveniles is unconstitutional, as seen in instances like Miller v. Alabama.

No-Harmony Crimes:

Sentencing Reform: A rising tide of opinion is calling for changes to sentencing rules that perpetuate the practice of life sentences for non-violent crimes, such as drug crimes or those subjected to the three strikes statute.

Conclusion

The effectiveness of life sentences as a deterrent against crime and the relative merits of rehabilitation and reintegration programs are ongoing topics of debate.

The death penalty is a major and harsh tool in the arsenal of nations that utilise it to deal with the gravest of crimes. Although it accomplishes the goals of punishment, dissuasion, immobilisation, and, occasionally, rehabilitation, it also brings up significant concerns regarding human rights and ethics. The utilisation of life imprisonment varies throughout legal systems due to persistent concerns regarding the care of inmates, the possibility of reform, and the equilibrium between punishment and rehabilitation.

28. Indefinite imprisonment

The term "indefinite imprisonment" refers to a type of sentencing in which the exact length of time a prisoner spends behind bars is not defined, but their release is subject to factors like rehabilitation, risk assessment, or concerns about the public's safety. People who are considered too dangerous to be released after serving a conventional sentence are commonly sentenced to indefinite incarceration, which differs from fixed-term punishments in that it does not have a predetermined end date.

Important Elements of Indefinite Detention Goals and Justifications:

"Public Safety" means keeping people out of harm's way when they are judged to be a persistent danger to the community.

Giving people the chance to get back on their feet and rejoin society safely is what we mean when we talk about rehabilitation.

The ability to continuously evaluate and modify according to the person's actions and risk level is an example of legal flexibility.

Conditions and Legal Framework:

The sentencing process is usually reserved for the most heinous of offences or for those whose recidivism rates are very high.

Parole boards or equivalent entities evaluate each parolee on a regular basis to determine their level of risk and development.

The release process is conditional on the individual fulfilling certain requirements, such as proving they have rehabilitated or significantly reduced their risk.

Categories of Life Without Parole:

The concept of preventive detention allows certain jurisdictions to hold prisoners indefinitely, even after serving their original sentence, if they are determined to pose a danger to public safety.

Sentences that do not have a specific end date but typically include a minimum duration that must be served before being eligible for review are known as indeterminate sentences.

Views from Around the World

America:

Some states' sex offender statutes provide the indefinite civil commitment of convicted sex offenders who are considered a danger to society after finishing their prison terms.

In cases when release is not an option, a life sentence might have the same effect as an infinite prison term.

British Isles:

Indefinite incarceration of dangerous offenders was made possible by the 2005 introduction of the Imprisonment for Public Protection (IPP) system. People convicted under IPP are still behind bars even though the law was repealed in 2012.

For those who are considered a threat to themselves or others as a result of their mental condition, the Mental Condition Act permits indefinite incarceration.

Disagreements and Discussions

Problems with Human Rights:

Concerns regarding arbitrary and possibly unfair incarceration without a clear route to release arise with indefinite imprisonment.

Prolonged incarceration without a set release date violates the right to liberty, an essential human right.

Concerns Regarding Law and Ethics:

Maintaining justice requires due process, which includes making sure that the processes of sentencing, review, and release are open and fair.

The concept of proportionality in punishment must be considered alongside the necessity of maintaining public safety.

Punishment vs. Rehabilitation:

Rather than relying solely on punitive measures, advocates contend that the emphasis should be on rehabilitation and reintegration.

How well indefinite prison terms work to decrease recidivism and safeguard public safety is an ongoing topic of debate.

Mental Health:

It is critical to guarantee that people held under indefinite incarceration regimes have access to sufficient mental health treatment and support services. Patients should not be forgotten in Mental Institutions.

Conclusion

Striking a balance between the demands of public safety, individual rights, and rehabilitation makes indefinite imprisonment a complicated and controversial part of the criminal justice system. There are major ethical, legal, and human rights concerns, even though it provides protection. In order to find a fair and effective way to handle dangerous criminals, there is ongoing discussion and an effort to improve the system.

29. The "Three Strikes Law"

Offenders convicted of three or more major or violent offences are subject to heavier punishments under the "Three Strikes Law" system. These laws, which have their roots in the US, impose harsh punishments, such as life in prison, on those who commit a third major offence following the conviction of two earlier violent or serious felonies.

Principal Elements of the Three Strikes Law:

A third conviction for a violent or major crime carries a harsher punishment, frequently life in prison, known as the "Three Strikes" law.

When a person gets a second significant felony conviction, their sentences can be doubled or even increased in some jurisdictions.

Important Aspects:

Crimes That Qualify: This statute is usually applied to violent or major felonies like rape, murder, armed robbery, and specific types of aggravated assault.

Conviction History: In order to trigger the higher penalties, both of your past convictions must have been for qualifying offences.

Differences by State:

California: The Golden State is famous for its harsh Three Strikes Law, which originally called for a life sentence for any third offence but has since been limited to very serious or violent offences due to changes.

When Washington passed its Three Strikes Law in 1993, it was the first state to do so, and it applied only to severe felonies.

Other States: The Three Strikes Law has been enacted by a number of other states, each with its own set of requirements and punishments.

Justification and Goals Deterrence: Aims to discourage recidivism by making repeat offenders face harsh punishments for several significant offences.

Aims to safeguard society by eradicating repeat offenders from the neighbourhood.

The term "retribution" refers to a punitive strategy that makes sure criminals who commit the same crime again face harsher punishment.

Disputes and Rebuttals

Equal distribution:

Some people think that the Three Strikes Law is too severe, especially for third offences that aren't violent, such as drug possession or minor larceny.

Before amendments were passed, there were instances in California where people were given life terms for third offences that were not very serious.

Overcrowding in Prisons:

The statute has had a role in the dramatic rise in jail populations, which has worsened overcrowding and the expenses related to it.

The increasing number of lifers in states that have passed the Three Strikes Law has been a problem for these states.

Inequalities in Race and Class:

Evidence suggests that minority groups and people from lower socioeconomic backgrounds are disproportionately impacted by the law.

These disparities are exacerbated by differences in the prevalence of arrests, sentencing policies, and availability of legal aid.

Efficiency and Persistence:

There is conflicting evidence about the law's ability to reduce crime rates; some studies find little influence on recidivism after release, while others find no effect on deterrence at all.

Rehabilitative and preventative strategies, rather than harsh punitive ones, are advocated by critics.

Alterations and Reforms Proposition 36 of 2012 in the State of California:

Reworked the Three Strikes Law to place a cap on life sentences for particularly violent or significant third offences.

Judgement:

The offender's criminal record and the specifics of the third offence are now factors that judges in certain jurisdictions can take into account when deciding on a sentence.

Programs for Alternative Sentencing:

Alternatives to jail for non-violent criminals, such as drug treatment programs and rehabilitation, should receive more attention.

Conclusion

A tough-on-crime strategy, the Three Strikes Law seeks to reduce recidivism and increase public safety. Concerns about equity, efficacy, and proportionality have prompted heated discussion about its implementation. Some areas have stuck to the old "three strikes" policy, while others have changed it to be more lenient and include rehabilitation in the sentencing process for repeat offenders. This discussion shows how important it is to have a fair and humane criminal justice system that also ensures public safety.

30. Parole

Parole allows a convicted felon to be released from jail on certain conditions before serving out their entire term. It permits the offender to serve the balance of their term in the community under supervision, with certain requirements. There should be less prison population, more opportunities for rehabilitation, and easier reintegration of parolees into society as a whole.

Important Elements of the Parole Procedure:

In most cases, an inmate's conduct and rehabilitation progress while behind bars, as well as the length and type of the offence, determine whether they are eligible for parole. However, this does not always hold across jurisdictions.

When deciding whether or not to grant parole, a parole board or comparable body examines the case of the prisoner. Inmates' prison behaviour, rehabilitation program participation, and societal danger are all aspects that are taken into account during this review.

The parole hearing is an opportunity for the inmate to argue for his or her release from prison. The prosecution and the victims may both get a chance to speak.

Parole Restrictions:

The purpose of parole supervision is to ensure that parolees are following the parole conditions and to help them reintegrate into society.

Common Requirements: Some common requirements include not contacting victims, not having firearms, not engaging in criminal activities, and keeping a job.

Additional requirements may include drug testing, curfew observance, or counselling, depending on the circumstances.

Parole Revocation:

The parolee is subject to re-incarceration if they disobey the terms of their release. The commission of new offences, the failure to pass drug tests, or the non-attendance at parole officer appointments are all examples of violations.

To decide whether a parolee should be sent back to jail, a hearing is normally scheduled for revocation. Parolees have the right to defend themselves against parole revocation by presenting evidence.

The goal of parole rehabilitation

The goal of parole rehabilitation is to increase the likelihood that incarcerated individuals will participate in and successfully complete rehabilitation programs to meet the requirements for parole.

Facilitates parolees' gradual readjustment to society through supervision and support, to lower the likelihood that they will reoffend.

Management of Correctional Facilities:

Assists in reducing jail populations by releasing offenders determined to be less of a danger to the general public.

There is a large gap in parole policy between the federal and state levels of government. When it comes to specific crimes, some states have done away with parole altogether, while others have kept or changed their systems.

In a mandatory parole program, an offender is automatically released after serving a specific percentage of their sentence, whereas in a discretionary parole program, the decision is made by a parole board.

England and Wales:

In the United Kingdom, parolees are said to be "on licence" when they are out on parole. Offenders who are granted a licence are expected to adhere to certain regulations while being monitored by probation officials.

Offenders serving indeterminate sentences are subject to risk assessments and rehabilitation evaluations in order to determine if they are eligible for parole release.

Australia:

The parole system in Australia is decentralised and operates independently in each of the country's states and territories.

Australian parole boards take the offender's conduct, the seriousness of the crime, and their rehabilitation initiatives into account when making decisions.

Canada:

Offenders can apply for parole after spending a certain amount of time, usually around a third of their sentence for most crimes.

Considerations including rehabilitation, public safety, and the offender's behaviour while incarcerated are considered by the Parole Board of Canada when making parole decisions.

Challenges and Debates

Public Safety:

Concerns about the risk posed by parolees to public safety, particularly in cases where parolees commit new crimes after release.

Rehabilitation vs. Punishment:

Balancing the goals of rehabilitation and punishment, with debates over the effectiveness of parole in achieving these goals.

Disparities and Fairness:

Addressing disparities in parole decisions, with concerns about consistency and fairness in the parole process.

Support and Resources:

Ensuring adequate support and resources for parolees to facilitate successful reintegration and reduce recidivism rates.

Conclusion

Parole is a crucial component of the criminal justice system, aimed at promoting rehabilitation, reducing prison populations, and facilitating the reintegration of offenders into society. While it offers significant benefits, including the potential for reduced recidivism and support for parolees, it also presents challenges related to public safety, fairness, and resource allocation. Ongoing reforms and evaluations are essential to balance these competing interests and enhance the effectiveness of parole systems globally.

31. Probation

Those who have been found guilty of a crime might alternatively opt to serve their sentence in the community under the watchful eye of a probation officer. Usually, a judge will approve it, and the criminal will have some requirements to meet before they can avoid jail.

Important Considerations for Probation Eligibility and Granting:

Factors that determine whether an offender is eligible for probation include the seriousness and type of the offence, the offender's prior criminal record, and the probability that they will be able to change their ways.

The suggestion of probation officers or other court officials, as well as the facts of the case, inform the judge's decision about the award of probation.

Probation Restrictions:

Regular appointments with a probation officer, continuing to work or attend school, not using drugs or alcohol, and not being involved in any illegal activities are common conditions.

Additional conditions may apply, such as community service, victim restitution, counselling or treatment program participation, travel restrictions, or prohibitions on associating with specific individuals.

How long is probation? It depends on the crime and the jurisdiction, but it usually ranges from a year or more.

Compliance and Supervision:

Officers on probation are responsible for keeping probationers accountable for their actions, ensuring that they are meeting their requirements, and reporting any infractions to the appropriate authorities.

Reviewing for Compliance:

It is usual practice to employ drug testing, home visits, and regular check-ins to guarantee adherence.

Infractions and Their Repercussions:

If a probationer commits a minor infringement, such as failing to appear for a scheduled appointment, the probation officer may issue a warning or impose stricter supervision.

Revocation of probation and reinstatement of the previous prison term or other sanctions may result from serious infractions, such as the commission of new offences. To decide whether probation should be revoked, a hearing is usually held. The probationer is entitled to provide proof and contest the revocation by arguing their case.

Views from Other Countries

United States of America:

Probation is a widely used alternative to jail for a variety of offences in both the federal and provincial systems.

State and municipal agencies usually oversee probation services, although their regulations and methods can differ.

England and Wales:

Community Orders: Probation is a component of community orders, which encompass a wider range of sanctions, including rehabilitation programs, curfews, and unpaid labour.

The National Probation Service is in charge of supervision and assistance for ex-offenders, and it is also responsible for managing probation services.

Australia:

Methods at the State Level: The probation system, including its requirements and processes, varies from one state or territory to another.

As part of community corrections, which encompasses a range of alternatives to incarceration and types of monitoring, probation is frequently administered.

Canada:

A sentence of probation may be imposed alone or in addition to additional sanctions, such as fines or community service, depending on the circumstances.

Various methods and programs are implemented by the various provincial and territory administrations in charge of probation services.

Justifications for Probation

Offenders are encouraged to participate in constructive activities and behaviours that aid in their rehabilitation and reintegration into society as part of the rehabilitation process.

Efficient Use of Resources: Decreases the expenses linked to incarceration by enabling supervised release from the community for offenders.

Provides an alternative to incarceration for appropriate criminals, thus helping to decrease prison overpopulation.

Offenders can participate in restorative justice programs that offer them chances to serve their communities, pay reparations, and engage in other forms of rehabilitation.

Difficulties and Controversies

Questions regarding probation's ability to guarantee long-term behavioural change and decrease recidivism rates have prompted this discussion.

The distribution of resources should be such that probation officers can adequately supervise and assist probationers with reasonable caseloads.

Being consistent and fair:

Addressing disparities: Probation can be granted or revoked depending on the judge's discretion, the jurisdiction, and the specifics of each case.

Racism, social status, and other forms of prejudice must not be considered in probation judgements.

Assistance and Recovery:

Making sure that probationers can get their hands on the education, counselling, and job training they need is an important part of providing them with access to services.

Substance Abuse and Mental Health: Providing individualised services to probationers who are struggling with substance abuse or mental health difficulties.

Security for the General Population:

Making sure that probation is used properly for low-risk offenders is one way to strike a balance between the interests of rehabilitation and public safety.

Conclusion

An essential part of our criminal justice system, probation provides an alternative to jail that prioritises rehabilitation, efficiency, and reintegration into society. Reducing jail overcrowding and helping ex-offenders reintegrate into society are two of its many positive aspects, but it also has problems with efficiency, equity, and resource distribution. Improving the efficacy and equity of probation systems worldwide requires continuous evaluations and improvements.

32. Life in Prison in England, including Wales.

The death penalty, life in prison without the possibility of parole, and other capital punishments are reserved for the most heinous of crimes in England and Wales, including terrorism, murder, and specific sexual and violent offences. Although this is not necessarily the case, a life sentence does suggest that the perpetrator will be subject to the sentence indefinitely. A variety of life sentences are available, each with its own set of parole eligibility requirements and procedures.

Various Forms of Life Sentences

Minimum Life Requirement:

The death penalty is in place in England and Wales for the crime of murder. A life sentence is the punishment for a murder conviction.

The Life Sentence: A Judicial Decision

Life sentences are handed down by judges with discretion, depending on the gravity of the act and the offender's prior convictions, for other heinous crimes including manslaughter, rape, or armed robbery.

Lifetime Sentence:

An offender given a whole life sentence cannot be released from jail at any point during their incarceration. Only the most horrific acts, including those involving multiple murders or those driven by political motives, merit this punishment.

Two Types of Sentences: Determinate and Indeterminate

Tariff Minimum Term:

If a judge hands down a life sentence without the possibility of parole, the offender must serve at least the minimum time (tariff) before being released. The severity of the crime, any aggravating or mitigating circumstances, and the Sentencing Council's recommendations all go into determining the tariff. Parole is an option for offenders who have served the minimum sentence, but it does not ensure release.

Sentence Lacking Clarity:

With an indeterminate sentence, the offender's release date is up in the air; instead, the court can decide how long to keep them behind bars. The Parole Board must determine whether the parolee poses a danger to society before granting parole.

Decision on Parole and Release:

The criminal is eligible to seek parole after serving the mandatory minimum sentence. If the parolee is considered a danger to society, the Parole Board will grant their release.

Offender conduct in jail, rehabilitation program attendance, psychological testing, and risk assessments are all factors.

Restrictions on Parole:

If parole is granted, the parolee will be subject to stringent requirements, such as regular appointments with a probation officer, electronic monitoring, mobility restrictions, and rehabilitation program participation requirements.

If the perpetrator does not adhere to these terms, they may be sent back to prison.

License Life Sentence:

The parolee's license is valid for the rest of their life. If they fail to comply with their parole terms or commit another crime, they will be subject to immediate revocation of their parole and remand to prison.

Permanent Restrictions

Standards for the Imposition of Lifetime Orders:

Extremely heinous offences, such as several killings, kidnapping and sexual assault involving a minor, murder committed for ideological, religious, or political reasons, or a prior murder conviction, warrant whole life sentences.

Evaluation of Lifetime Sentences:

Although reviews of whole-life sentences are uncommon, defendants do have the option to appeal their sentencing or seek a review in response to newly discovered evidence or legislative changes.

Guidelines and Legal Framework

Sentencing recommendations: Judges can refer to the Sentencing Council's recommendations for minimum life sentences, which take into consideration the gravity of the offence, any mitigating or aggravating circumstances, and any legislative requirements.

Human Rights Considerations: The ECHR and other human rights norms must be followed by life sentences, especially entire life orders. Within the framework of life sentences, questions of hope, humane treatment, and proportionality are examined.

New Information and Controversies

Healing and Readjustment:

The usefulness of life sentences as a deterrent, the appropriateness of rehabilitation programs, and the resources required to help ex-offenders reintegrate into society are all topics of continuing discussion.

The Reforms to Sentencing:

Fair and uniform application of life sentences that reflect changing societal values and legal norms is the goal of periodic evaluations and changes.

Managing Risks and Ensuring Public Safety:

The administration of life sentences presents a primary challenge: maintaining public safety while allowing offenders who no longer constitute a threat the chance for rehabilitation and eventual release.

Conclusion

In England and Wales, life sentences are reserved for the most heinous of crimes, striking a balance between the competing goals of public safety, justice, and rehabilitation. Life sentences show a complex approach to criminal justice because they guarantee the eradication of dangerous offenders from society but also include review and parole procedures. Life sentences are still a topic of heated controversy, with revisions and ongoing debates aiming to bring them in line with modern notions of justice and human rights.

33. Criminal Justice

All the rules and regulations put in place by various governments to keep the peace, make sure everyone pays what they have to pay, and ensure that everyone gets what they deserve are collectively known as the criminal justice system. Its stated goals include reducing criminal activity, punishing lawbreakers, and establishing a level playing field for all citizens. Several departments and procedures make up the system, such as the police, courts, and prisons.

The Criminal Justice System's Essential Elements
Enforcement of the Law:

Law enforcement officers are tasked with enforcing laws, preventing crime, capturing criminals, and ensuring public order.

The Federal Bureau of Investigations (FBI) in the US and the United Kingdom's Serious Fraud Office are two examples of investigative agencies that focus on particular crimes.

An approach to police work known as "community policing" emphasizes fostering mutual trust and collaboration between residents and police officers.

The Courts:

Judgement of matters, interpretation of laws, and the maintenance of an unbiased and fair legal procedure are all functions of the courts.

Magistrates and judges: Have the authority to decide cases, hand down penalties, and preside over court procedures.

Prosecutors: Criminal trials are handled by prosecutors who represent the state or government; to provide evidence and bring charges against those who have committed crimes.

Legal Council: Professional lawyers like barristers and solicitors who specialize in defence law represent those facing criminal charges by laying forth their legal options and defending their clients' rights.

Correctional Systems:

Institutions that house inmates while they await trial or serve out sentences for criminal offences are known as prisons and jails.

Parole and Probation: Alternatives to jail that enable parolees and probationers to fulfil their sentences in the community under supervision.

Education, vocational training, counselling, and drug addiction treatment are the main tenets of rehabilitation programs, which aim to reform ex-offenders.

Investigations in the Criminal Justice System:

As soon as someone contacts the police to report a crime, the procedure can start.

Conducting an investigation entails collecting evidence, questioning potential witnesses, and naming potential perpetrators.

To make an arrest, one must have evidence and probable cause to bring a suspect to justice.

The process of charging:

The decision to press charges is based on the prosecution's examination of the evidence.

Formal charges are brought before the court and the accused is apprised of the accusations throughout this process.

Before the Trial:

The accused must first appear before a judge, who will then set bail and any other terms associated with it.

The purpose of the preliminary hearing is to ascertain whether or not the evidence is sufficient to move forward with the trial.

To settle a matter out of court, the prosecution and defence may engage in plea bargaining negotiations.

Trial:

If a jury is needed to hear the case, they will be chosen at the beginning of this process.

Prosecutors and defendants each give opening statements outlining their case to the jury.

Witnesses and evidence are presented and examined by both the prosecution and the defence.

During closing arguments, attorneys for both sides restate their positions and make one last plea to the judge or jury.

The judge or jury finds the defendant guilty or innocent.

Passage of sentence:

If the offender is found guilty, a sentencing hearing will be conducted to decide on a suitable sentence.

When deciding on a sentence, judges frequently go to established statutes for guidance.

Possible Penalties: Jail, community service, fines, probation, or other forms of restorative justice may be imposed.

Submit an appeal:

The person found guilty often has the legal right to request a rehearing of their case.

Appellate Courts: These courts look for mistakes made by the lower court in terms of the law.

Purposes of the Criminal Process

As a kind of retribution, the offence must be punished with punishments commensurate with its gravity.

Rehabilitation: Changing criminals so they don't commit crimes again.

For public safety, incapacitating somebody means removing them from society.

Repairing the harm that criminal behaviour brings about is known as restoration. This generally involves making restitution to victims and performing community service.

Problems and Obstacles

Prisons and jails frequently experience overcrowding, which results in unsanitary conditions and heightened conflicts among inmates.

Arrest, sentencing, and penitentiary rates are skewed by racial, socioeconomic, and gender inequalities.

Conflicting views persist on how best to balance the aims of rehabilitation with those of punitive actions.

In order to successfully rehabilitate offenders, it is essential to attend to their mental health requirements.

Efficacious rehabilitation and support programs can reduce recidivism.

New Approaches and Changes

By bringing together ex-offenders and current victims, restorative justice seeks to heal the wounds inflicted by criminal behaviour.

Offenders can be redirected from the conventional criminal justice system to alternative programs that focus on treatment or education through diversion programs.

Reducing the need for jail and making sentences more equal are the goals of sentencing reforms.

Improvements in jail procedures, court administration, and law enforcement were made possible by technological advancements.

Crime prevention and rehabilitation programs that include community members are known as community-based initiatives.

Conclusion

When it comes to enforcing laws and keeping society in order, the criminal justice system is indispensable. It is a multi-process, multi-stakeholder system that is always changing. There will always be questions and arguments about how best to achieve the purposes of rehabilitation, public safety, punishment, and deterrence. Addressing these difficulties and improving the criminal justice system's effectiveness, fairness, and humanity requires continuous improvements and innovations.

34. Habitual Offender

Anyone with a lengthy record of convictions is considered a career criminal, chronic offender, or repeat offender. These criminals frequently display a pattern of illegal behaviour by engaging in continuous or repetitive illicit behaviour. Laws and practices concerning repeat offenders differ from one jurisdiction to the next, however, it's common for many legal systems to penalise repeat offenders more severely.

Important Ideas Concerning the Recidivism of Habitual Offenders:

Recidivism is the propensity of a convicted offender to commit new crimes. Because of their high recidivism rates, criminal justice strategies target habitual offenders to decrease the number of offences they commit.

Quantification: The frequency of re-arrests, re-convictions, or re-incarcerations within a given time frame following release is a common metric for determining recidivism rates.

Rules & Regulations:

"Three Strikes" Laws: People convicted of three or more major crimes face harsh punishments, including life in prison, under "three strikes" laws in some jurisdictions, including some US states.

The purpose of enhanced sentencing is to prevent further criminal behaviour and ensure the public's safety by imposing lengthier or harsher terms on repeat offenders.

Standards for Categorization:

The number and type of convictions a person has usually determines whether they are considered a habitual offender. If a person has three felony convictions, for instance, they may be considered a habitual offender.

Crime Type: Habitual offender status is more common among those who commit violent offences, drug trafficking, or significant property crimes.

Foundational Law and Illustrative Cases

United States of America:

Offenders found guilty of three or more egregious crimes are required by law to serve life terms under the "Three Strikes" statute, which is in effect in many states (including California).

The number of past convictions and the severity of punishment for repeat offenders are determined by various state statutes that establish harsher sentencing for habitual offenders.

England and Wales:

The term "persistent offender" is used to describe repeat criminals in the United Kingdom. According to the Criminal Justice Act of 2003, a person's prior convictions can be taken into account by the courts when sentencing them, and those who commit the same crime more than once may be subject to harsher punishments.

Australia:

Serious Repeat Offenders: Laws aimed at serious repeat offenders have been enacted by many states and territories. For some repeat offences, for example, Western Australia's legislation provides mandatory minimum terms.

Canada:

A person can be given an indeterminate sentence in Canada if they are designated as a dangerous offender. This means that they can be imprisoned in jail indefinitely if society believes they continue to pose a threat to society.

Problems and Rebuttals

Effectiveness: When it comes to deterrence, people aren't sure that tougher punishments for repeat offenders work. It is not always the case that longer sentences decrease recidivism rates, according to certain research.

Proponents of rehabilitation say that penalising offenders does little to help them overcome problems like substance misuse, mental illness, and a lack of educational and occupational possibilities, which they say are the root causes of criminal behaviour.

Justness and Equilibrium:

Concerns regarding justice and fairness arise from the fact that enhanced sentencing regulations, such as three-strikes laws, might result in excessively lengthy penalties for very few offences.

Disparities in Race and Income: Policies targeting repeat offenders have the potential to exacerbate racial and economic disparities by imposing harsher penalties on already vulnerable populations.

Money and Materials:

Overcrowding in Prisons: The use of longer prison terms for repeat criminals puts a burden on correctional facilities' capacity to house inmates.

Fiscal Burden: Long-term incarceration of repeat criminals is expensive for society and takes resources away from initiatives that could reduce crime and help rehabilitated ex-offenders lead productive lives.

Projects for Change and Alternatives Diversion:

Drug courts and mental health courts are two examples of problem-solving courts that aim to provide alternatives to jail by treating the underlying reasons for criminal behaviour.

Programs that provide rigorous community supervision and support can help reduce recidivism among repeat offenders.

Programs for Rehabilitation and Reintegration:

Offenders can be better prepared for reintegration into society and have a lower risk of recidivism if they receive education and vocational training.

Treatment for substance addiction: When it comes to breaking the cycle of repeated crime, it can be vital to address substance addiction issues through treatment programs.

The Reforms to Sentencing:

Concerns about justice and fairness can be alleviated by reforms that try to make sure that penalties are proportional to the seriousness of the crime and the offender's criminal record.

Tools for Assessing Risk: Offenders who are at high risk to society and those who would benefit most from rehabilitation can be located with the use of evidence-based risk assessment tools.

Conclusion

Stricter punishments for habitual offenders are an attempt to reduce criminal behaviour by individuals who commit the same crime regularly. Problems with efficacy, equity, and resource allocation arise, even though these measures can improve public safety by rendering dangerous criminals unable to harm others. Finding a middle ground between punishment, rehabilitation, and deterrence is essential for fair and successful methods of dealing with repeat offenders. Recidivism can be reduced and outcomes for offenders and society improved through reforms that target the underlying reasons of criminal behaviour and offer assistance for reintegration.

35. Miscarriage of Justice

A miscarriage of justice happens when mistakes or shortcomings in the criminal justice system lead to an unfair conviction or legal result. This can occur when a guilty defendant is acquitted or when an innocent person is convicted, or in any case when a fair and just outcome cannot be reached through the judicial system. To restore public trust, reforms must be implemented continuously.

Unjust Convictions: What Leads to Miscarriages of Justice?

False confessions: Wrongful convictions can result from coerced or false confessions obtained through harsh or inappropriate interrogation procedures.

The most common reason for erroneous convictions is a mistake in eyewitness identification. This mistake might be caused by faulty recall or by using suggestive identification processes.

Inadequate Defence: Wrongful convictions can occur as a result of inadequate legal counsel, which is frequently caused by underfunded public defender systems or professional ineptitude.

False evidence presented, witness tampering, or withholding of exculpatory evidence are all examples of prosecutorial misconduct that can result in unjust convictions.

Wrongful convictions can occur when police officers engage in misconduct during investigations. This includes practices like fabricating evidence or pressuring witnesses.

Wrongful convictions can occur as a result of forensic errors, which include faulty DNA testing or the utilisation of outdated forensic methodologies.

Broad Problems:

Unfair treatment and erroneous convictions can result from prejudice and discrimination based on gender, race, socioeconomic status, and other characteristics.

Unfair results can occur when judges make mistakes when interpreting the law or conducting trials.

Miscarriages of justice can occur as a result of faulty legal procedures, such as an inadequate review process or an absence of an appeals process.

What Happens When People Are Incorrectly Convicted:

Freedom Lost: Unjust imprisonment can rob wrongfully convicted people of years—if not decades—of their lives.

Trauma to the Mind and Emotions: Being falsely convicted and imprisoned can cause a great deal of mental and emotional distress.

Costs to Society and the Economy: People who are wrongfully convicted frequently have enormous obstacles when trying to start over, such as a lack of affordable housing and jobs.

Society and Victims:

People lose faith in the criminal justice system when they see wrongful convictions.

Crimes Go Unpunished: The real offenders behind these crimes can end up free, which keeps the public in danger.

Significant financial costs can arise from miscarriages of justice, such as compensating the erroneously convicted and covering expenses associated with retrials and inquiries.

Judgement Erosion

The Birmingham Six (UK):

Due to evidence of police pressure and concealment of exonerating evidence, six men were erroneously found guilty for the 1974 Birmingham pub bombings and were sentenced to 16 years in jail. Eventually, their convictions were reversed.

American Steven Avery: Avery was wrongfully convicted of sexual assault and attempted murder and spent 18 years behind bars before DNA evidence cleared his name. His later murder conviction, which was covered in the documentary "Making a Murderer," has also brought up serious concerns over possible injustices.

American Joyce Gilchrist: A forensic chemist whose false and misleading evidence led to multiple erroneous convictions. The revelation of her wrongdoing prompted a reassessment of forensic procedures and several exonerations.

Reforms in the Law to Avoid and Resolve Miscarriages of Justice:

Better Access to Legal Defence: Making sure everyone, especially those without means, can afford a qualified defence attorney.

Forensic analysis should be subject to strict regulations and control to reduce the likelihood of mistakes and wrongdoing.

Increased openness and responsibility on the part of law enforcement, prosecutors, and judges through the adoption of new policies and procedures.

Advocacy and Innocence Projects:

Innocence Projects: Groups whose mission is to use legal and scientific methods, with a concentration on DNA evidence, to investigate and free falsely convicted individuals.

Public Education Efforts: In order to get support for changes, it is necessary to educate the public on the reasons for and effects of false convictions.

Control and Evaluation Procedures:

Miscarriages of justice and allegations of wrongful convictions can be investigated by establishing independent review boards.

To find and fix systemic problems, it is necessary to do audits of forensic labs and criminal cases on a regular basis.

Prohibited Measures:

The right to appeal a conviction must be solidly in place and easily available for anyone who believes they have been wrongfully convicted.

Providing avenues for persons to seek reevaluation and relief based on fresh evidence or legal arguments constitutes access to post-conviction remedies.

Conclusion

Individuals and society suffer greatly when the criminal justice system fails to prevent miscarriages of justice. Several steps are needed to solve these problems, such as changes to the law, better forensic procedures, more openness and responsibility, and funding for advocacy groups. Criminal justice will be fairer if it finds out why people are wrongfully convicted and then does something about it.

36. Pardon

An individual is entirely released from the legal ramifications of a criminal conviction when they receive a pardon, which is a type of executive clemency. It can be issued either before or after conviction and is usually bestowed by a head of state or high-ranking government official like a president, governor, or monarch. Pardons are commonly viewed as gestures of charity, forgiveness, or the rectifying of court mistakes; however, they do not automatically indicate innocence.

Pardon Categories:

Full Pardon:

It absolves the offender of full responsibility for the crime and eliminates any punishments or restrictions related to it.

A conditional pardon comes with certain requirements that the forgiven person must fulfil, such as serving time in the community or being on probation.

After a person has passed away, a posthumous pardon can be granted, typically to make up for wrongs done in the past.

A Pardon's Impact:

As far as the law is concerned, a pardon usually reinstates civil rights that have been lost as a result of a conviction. These rights include the ability to vote, run for public office, and serve on a jury.

Although a pardon formally absolves the offender of criminal responsibility, the stigmatisation that has developed as a result of their conviction may persist.

Documentation:

A pardon may indicate that a conviction has been pardoned, but it does not remove the conviction itself from a person's criminal record.

Procedure and Power:

A detailed application outlining the applicant's situation and the grounds for requesting clemency is typically required of those seeking pardons.

Review:

An advisory group or pardon board will usually look over the application and advise the person who gives the pardon.

The discretion to give or refuse the pardon ultimately lies with the issuing authority, be it the president, the governor, or the monarch.

Various Jurisdictions in the US Shown by Pardon Examples:

The power to pardon for federal offences rests with the President of the United States. The pardoning of Richard Nixon by President Gerald Ford and the commuting of sentences for many nonviolent drug offenders by President Barack Obama are two prominent examples.

Pardons for State offences:

The power to pardon state offences rests with the governor. Pardon processes and requirements differ from one state to another.

England and Wales:

The ability to pardon is a royal prerogative that the king exercises in consultation with government ministers. When necessary, such as to rectify a humanitarian crisis or a miscarriage of justice, this power is used.

Canada:

The Parole Board of Canada grants a record suspension.

Australia:

The power to pardon for federal offences rests with the Governor-General, while state governors hold the same ability.

Dilemmas and Problems

How Pardons Are Abused:

Pardons have the potential to be utilised as a kind of political favouritism, intending to reward political followers or friends at the expense of the integrity of the legal system.

Pardon procedures are not always open and public, which raises concerns about justice and responsibility.

Effect on Fairness:

Injustices Can Be Corrected: Pardons can be used to fix wrongfully convicted people and rectify wrongs from the past.

How the Public Views the System: Pardons have the power to change how the public views the criminal justice system. They can either strengthen faith in the system's capacity to rectify mistakes or weaken trust when seen as unfair or arbitrary.

Consequences for Society and the Law:

Pardons help ex-offenders reintegrate into society by restoring their rights and lowering their barriers to employment and social acceptance.

Social stigma and difficulties stemming from prior convictions may persist even after a legal pardon.

Pardons of Note

One of the most contentious pardons in American history was that of Richard Nixon, the previous president, by President Gerald Ford, for any transgressions that may have occurred during the Watergate crisis.

English mathematician and WWII codebreaker Alan Turing was posthumously pardoned in 2013 for his 1952 conviction for homosexuality, which was a crime at the time.

Conclusion

The criminal justice system's powerful instrument, a pardon, allows for forgiveness, the repair of court mistakes, and the restoration of rights. Although it is essential in helping those who have served their time or who have been unfairly convicted, it is also fraught with the risk of abuse and controversy. The public's faith and respect for the ideals of justice depend on a pardoning procedure that is open, honest, and equitable.

37. Recidivism

The propensity for a person with a criminal record to re-offend and engage in criminal activity is known as recidivism.

Recidivism rates that are high show that the root reasons of criminal behaviour have not been adequately addressed, whereas rates that are low show that the treatments have been successful.

Important Elements That Lead to Recidivism

Unemployment and Low Levels of Education: Because of the challenges in obtaining steady employment and reintegrating into society, individuals with poor education and job skills are more prone to recidivism.

Drug Misuse:

Many incarcerated individuals continue to battle with substance addiction difficulties after their release, which is a major factor in their recidivism.

Stress and Mental Illness:

Persistent criminal activity may result from untreated mental health disorders. A lot of people who commit crimes have mental health issues that need to be addressed and supported.

Economic and Social Considerations:

Many formerly incarcerated people face significant obstacles to reintegration into society, including financial hardship, unstable housing, and limited social support networks.

Missing Rehab Opportunities:

To reduce the likelihood of recidivism, it is essential that high-quality rehabilitation programs be available both during and after incarceration. Educational, occupational, and behavioural therapy programs are crucial.

Policy on Criminal Justice:

By reducing parole and rehabilitation options, policies like three strikes laws and mandatory minimum terms can increase recidivism rates.

Assessing the Rate of Recidivism through Arrests, re-convictions and reincarcerations:

The frequency of re-arrests for previously freed individuals for different offences.

The frequency of re-convictions for previously released felons.

The frequency with which ex-offenders are re-incarcerated, either for fresh crimes or for failing to comply with release terms (such as parole infractions).

Programs for Education and Job Training to Reduce Recidivism:

Giving people the chance to get a degree and learn a trade can help them find a job and become productive members of society again.

Help for Substance Misuse:

Inmates and community members alike can benefit from comprehensive drug misuse treatment programs in their fight against criminal behaviour.

Services for Mental Health:

Reoffending is less likely to occur when people with mental illnesses have access to treatment and support.

Programs for Reentry

Successful reintegration requires programs that aid inmates in navigating the community after release from jail, such as those that connect them with housing, jobs, and social services.

Assistance and Oversight in the Community:

Recidivism can be reduced by the use of effective probation and parole systems that offer supervision, assistance, and resources.

Programs for Restorative Justice:

By getting to the heart of why people commit crimes in the first place, restorative justice strategies that prioritise job creation instead of outsourcing jobs to other countries, fostering understanding, and involving the community might help cut down on recidivism.

Personalised Methods of Help:

Recidivism can be reduced more effectively through programs and interventions that are customised to meet the unique requirements and mitigate the risks faced by each offender.

Prominent Projects and Programs

In the US, there is the Second Chance Act:

Reentry services, job aid, and drug addiction treatment are all part of a federal law that tries to lower the rate of recidivism.

System of Corrections in Norway:

The jail system in Norway boasts one of the world's lowest recidivism rates, because of its emphasis on rehabilitation and compassionate treatment. It emphasises reintegration assistance, vocational training, and education.

Hawaii's HOPE Probation Program:

Success in lowering recidivism has been achieved by a probation program that offers substance addiction treatment and assistance in addition to using swift and specific sanctions for infractions.

Recidivism Reduction Obstacles: Limited Resources

Reentry and rehabilitation programs may struggle to launch or remain operational due to a lack of resources and financing.

Political Will and Public Perception:

It might be particularly difficult to change public opinion and gain governmental backing for rehabilitation strategies in settings that value punishment.

Interagency Cooperation:

Reintegration programs can only be successful if the many organisations and agencies that make up the criminal justice system work together effectively.

Conclusion

Rehabilitation, support, and removing causes of criminal behaviour are essential components of any complete strategy to reduce recidivism. Societies can improve public safety, decrease jail costs, and increase individual and community outcomes by reinvesting in education, job training, mental health services, and reentry programs and altering criminal justice policies.

38 Penology, Rehabilitation

Offenders' reintegration into society and prevention of further criminal behaviour are the primary goals of rehabilitation programs in the field of penology. To reduce recidivism and promote public safety, rehabilitation programs aim to treat the root reasons of criminal behaviour, which might include mental health disorders, substance misuse, and a lack of education.

Rehabilitation Education and Training Essential Elements

Programs for Education:

Inmates have access to basic literacy classes, and possibilities for further education so that they can gain valuable life skills.

To increase employability upon release, vocational training is provided in fields such as plumbing, carpentry, culinary arts, and technology.

Drug and Alcohol Rehabilitation

In-Prison Programs:

Extensive programs are designed to assist individuals in overcoming addiction while they are incarcerated.

Recovery and prevention of recurrence are the goals of aftercare services, which provide ongoing assistance and therapy following discharge. These services might help those who are willing to participate.

Services for Mental Health

Evaluation and Treatment:

Conducting mental health screenings, delivering effective therapy, and overseeing medication management.

Inmate mental health counselling and support groups are available as support services.

Treatment for Behavioural Issues

Inmates can benefit from programs that teach them to think and act in more positive ways through cognitive behavioural therapy (CBT).

Prisoners can learn to regulate their anger and find peaceful solutions to disagreements through anger management classes.

Alternative Dispute Resolution Models

Mediating sessions between perpetrators and victims to foster mutual understanding and healing is known as victim-offender mediation.

As a component of their rehabilitation, felons are often required to participate in community service projects.

Skills for Daily Living

Inmates can learn to budget, save, and handle their own finances through financial literacy programs.

Parenting Classes: Inmates will learn about parenting and their roles as parents.

Reentry Services

Customised reintegration plans that take into account each person's unique requirements in terms of housing, work, and medical care are known as transition plans.

Helping formerly incarcerated people readjust to society after release through the provision of supervision and other forms of probation and parole support.

Positive Outcomes from Rehabilitation: Decreased Recidivism

Promoting public safety, in the long run, is possible through reducing the chance of recidivism by dealing with the underlying reasons for criminal behaviour.

Saving Money

The financial burden on society and the criminal justice system is diminished when the recidivism rate is decreased.

Public Safety is Enhanced

Community safety is enhanced when formerly incarcerated individuals are less likely to re-offend.

Advantages for Society

By treating criminals with respect and dignity, rehabilitation emphasizes their capacity for personal development and atonement.

Better Communities and Stronger Families

When formerly incarcerated people can successfully reintegrate into society, it can have a positive impact on both families and communities.

Problems with Efficient Rehabilitation Due to Limited Resources

Inadequate financing and resources can make it difficult to design and execute all-encompassing rehabilitation programs.

Political and Public Backing

It could be difficult to win over the public and politicians in settings that value punishment over rehabilitation when trying to implement such a strategy.

Regularity and High-Caliber

Maintaining a good standard of care while delivering rehabilitation programs at several facilities is not always easy.

Obstacles in the System

Rehabilitation that works must take a long-term, all-encompassing approach to tackle fundamental problems like racial and socioeconomic inequality.

Rehabilitation Program Examples

The Penal System in Norway

Rehabilitation and decent treatment are hallmarks of Norway's penal system. Recidivism rates are low at facilities like Halden Prison because of the emphasis on therapy, vocational training, and education.

PROBATION HOPE in Hawaii

The goal of this program is to decrease recidivism among high-risk offenders by providing them with treatment and assistance for substance addiction issues in addition to rapid and certain punishment for probation violations.

Project Entrepreneurship in Prisons (PEP) (USA)

Inmates can get the commercial and entrepreneurial skills they need to launch their own ventures when they leave prison thanks to PEP's training programs.

Conclusion

In penology, rehabilitation is essential for getting to the bottom of why people commit crimes in the first place and helping them successfully reintegrate into society. Recidivism, public safety, and individual and community results can all be improved through rehabilitation programs that emphasise education, vocational training, substance abuse treatment, mental health care, and life skills. Despite obstacles, a more equitable and efficient criminal justice system can only be achieved by sustained funding and advocacy for rehabilitation programs.

39. Restorative Justice

Restorative justice is an approach to justice that focuses on the rehabilitation of offenders through reconciliation with victims and the community at large. It emphasizes repairing the harm caused by criminal behaviour and seeks to bring together all stakeholders to find a resolution that promotes healing and reparation.

Key Principles of Restorative Justice

Repairing Harm: The primary goal is to address and repair the harm caused by the crime, both to the victims and the community.

Involvement of Stakeholders: Encourages the participation of victims, offenders, and community members in the justice process.

Accountability: Offenders are motivated to comprehend the consequences of their conduct and accept accountability for their acts.

Reconciliation and Reintegration: Focuses on the reconciliation of relationships and reintegration of the offender into the community.

Processes in Restorative Justice

Victim-Offender Mediation:

Description: Facilitated meetings between the victim and the offender to discuss the impact of the crime and agree on a way to repair the harm.

Benefits: Provides a platform for victims to express their feelings and needs, and for offenders to apologize and make amends.

Family Group Conferencing:

Description: Involves the offender, the victim, and their families or support networks in a discussion facilitated by a trained mediator.

Benefits: Engages the support systems of both the victim and the offender to find a collective resolution.

Description: Community members, victims, and offenders participate in a circle discussion led by a facilitator to address the harm and decide on reparative actions.

Benefits: Encourages community involvement and collective decision-making.

Restorative Panels or Boards:

Description: A group of trained community volunteers meets with the offender to discuss the impact of the crime and develop a plan for making amends.

Benefits: Provides community-based solutions and oversight.

Conclusion

Restorative justice offers a holistic approach to addressing crime by focusing on repairing harm, involving all stakeholders, and promoting accountability and reconciliation. While there are challenges to its implementation, the benefits of reduced recidivism, victim satisfaction, and community engagement make it a valuable complement to traditional justice systems. Continued support, training, and integration efforts are essential for the broader adoption and success of restorative justice practices.

40. Sex Offender Registry

The purpose of a sex offender register is to allow law enforcement to keep tabs on people who have been found guilty of sex crimes. By making public and law enforcement access information about convicted sex offenders, these registers aim to improve public safety. Each jurisdiction's sex offender registry is unique in its requirements for registration, the information it collects, and how long of a time of registration is required.

For the sake of public safety, sex offender registry

Notify communities when convicted sex offenders are in the area so people can

take safety precautions.

Risk reduction:

Help keep convicted criminals from reoffending by making them aware that they are being watched.

The Police:

By keeping records of convicted offenders current, you may help law enforcement with sex crime investigations and prevention efforts.

Information Included in Sex Offender Registries and Their Important Features:

Names, aliases, DOBs, physical descriptions, and photos are examples of personally identifiable information.

Details on the person's residency, including their present and past addresses as well as their places of employment and school.

The details of the conviction include the type of offence, the date of conviction, and the punishment handed down.

What You Need to Know to Register:

After completing any kind of release from custody, including probation, parole, or prison, offenders are required to register.

Offenders must keep their information current at all times, including when there are changes (such as an address), and at regular intervals (e.g., once a year or quarterly).

How long does registration last?

The seriousness of the crime determines the length of time a person must be registered in certain countries' tiered systems. One case in point is:

Tier I: Registration is usually necessary for 10–15 years.

Tier II: A two-decade registration is necessary.

Lifetime registration is necessary for Tier III.

Everyone Can View:

Registries Open to the Public: With the use of online databases, several governments make some records accessible to anybody who wants to look them up.

Information that is not publicly available, such as the precise location, may be kept from anyone other than law authorities.

Disputes and Rebuttals Effectiveness:

The efficacy of sex offender registries in reducing public safety risks and recidivism is a topic of continuing controversy. Reducing sex offences may have a limited impact, according to some studies.

Unintended Repercussions:

A person's social standing can be severely damaged if they are a registered offender. This can lead to a lack of career opportunities, housing limitations, and social exclusion from society.

Rehabilitation and reintegration of ex-offenders may be impacted by these difficulties.

Reliability and Balance:

Data Accuracy: It could be difficult to guarantee that registry data is accurate and up-to-date.

The Offences' Scope: Some registries include names of people convicted of little crimes or consensual conduct, which raises concerns about equity and proportionality, according to critics.

Legal Obstacles:

Concerns with Due Process, Privacy Violations, and Ex Post Facto Laws (Punishment after the fact) have led to legal challenges to registries, raising concerns about their constitutionality.

U.S. Sex Offender Registry Examples:

The United States keeps an extensive database of sex offenders, and websites such as the National Sex Offender Public Website (NSOPW) make this database accessible to the public.

North America:

The RCMP is responsible for maintaining Canada's National Sex Offender Registry, which is a database that law enforcement agencies can use to find information about convicted sex offenders.

England and Wales:

There are various limitations on the public dissemination of the sex offender registry that is maintained by police forces in the United Kingdom. Offenders have a responsibility to inform law enforcement whenever their situation changes.

Australia:

Registration procedures and timeframes differ by state in Australia's National Child Offender System (NCOS), which tracks those convicted of offences against children.

Conclusion

To improve public safety, sex offender registries keep tabs on people who have been found guilty of sex offences. Although they intend to aid law enforcement and the public, there are serious concerns about their efficacy, equity, and the possible negative effects on criminals' rehabilitation that they fail to address. Policymakers continue to face the significant task of finding a balance between public safety advantages, offenders' rights, and their chances of reintegration.

41. Sexually violent predator laws

The purpose of sexually violent predator (SVP) legislation is to deal with those who have committed serious sexual offences and are believed to be a continuing danger of committing additional violent sexual crimes. After serving their time in prison, these criminals might be "civilly committed" to treatment centres that meet certain criteria. Making sure offenders get the help they need while still protecting the public is the top priority.

Sexually Violent Predator

People convicted of heinous sexual offences like rape, child molestation, or violent sexual assaults are usually considered to have committed severe offences.

Psychological or personality disorders that increase the offender's propensity to perpetrate sexually violent predatory activities must be identified in the risk assessment when a person is classified as a sexually violent predator (SVP).

Method for Civil Commitment:

To find out if they qualify for SVP classification and how likely they are to re-offend, offenders undergo a psychiatric evaluation.

If the evaluation indicates that the offender may be subject to SVP status, the next step is to hold a court hearing. At this hearing, both the judge and the jury will consider the evidence and decide whether the criminal should be civilly committed.

Offenders found to have Significant Offender Profiles are obligated to attend a secure treatment centre for an unspecified amount of time, with frequent evaluations taking place.

Courses of Treatment:

Therapeutic Interventions: SVPs undergo rigorous mental and psychological therapy to lessen the likelihood that they will re-offend.

Ongoing reviews of the offender's risk and treatment progress are necessary to establish if release is safe.

Execution and Oversight:

Strict conditions may be imposed upon an offender's release from prison if it is determined that they no longer constitute a substantial danger.

Post-Release Supervision: Electronic monitoring, frequent check-ins, and compliance with specified criteria to guarantee public safety; ongoing monitoring.

U.S. Jurisdictional Examples of SVP Laws:

The United States Supreme Court's 1997 decision in Kansas v. Hendricks allowed for the legalisation of SVPs through civil commitment, which prompted several states to pass similar legislation.

Programs at the State Level: Stringent screening methods, commitment protocols, and specialised treatment programs are now mandated by SVP legislation in several states, including Washington, Florida, and California.

Canada:

In Canada, those who are considered to be a danger to society, such as sexual offenders, are subject to indeterminate penalties under the Dangerous Offender classification, which is similar to SVP statutes.

Australia:

Orders for Post-Sentence Monitoring: High-risk sexual offenders may be subject to post-sentence monitoring or incarceration in some Australian states.

Human Rights and Constitutional Concerns:

Concerns regarding double jeopardy and retroactive punishment have been voiced by critics of SVP laws, who contend that they effectively punish someone twice for the same offence.

Making sure that there are sufficient procedural safeguards to protect the rights of offenders during the civil commitment procedure is known as due process.

Efficiency and Morality:

The ethical responsibility to offer appropriate treatment and the possibility of rehabilitation must be considered alongside the necessity of public safety.

The Precision of Risk Assessments: Concerns regarding the validity and trustworthiness of risk assessment instruments employed to ascertain SVP status.

Distributing Resources:

Civil commitment programs, which include lodging, treatment, and monitoring of SVPs over an extended period of time, can incur significant implementation costs.

Correctional and Mental Health System Effects: Money and resources that are available for other criminal justice and mental health programs might change if SVP programs get more money.

Conclusion

To safeguard the general population from those who are judged to be a serious threat of perpetrating violent sexual offences, laws have been enacted to criminalise sexually violent predators. Balancing public safety with the need for rehabilitation is the goal of these laws, which involve the sentencing of high-risk criminals to secure treatment institutions.

42. Exoneration

The term "exoneration" refers to the official expungement of a criminal conviction when fresh evidence either proves the accused's innocence or shows that a major mistake was made during the trial. A vital part of the criminal justice system, exoneration seeks to rectify false convictions and provide fairness for those who have been falsely accused and penalised.

Identity Theft as a Root Cause of Wrongful Conviction:

One of the most common reasons for erroneous convictions is the mistake in witness identification. Many factors can distract a witness, including the stress of being a crime scene investigator, bad lighting, and the presence of firearms.

Untruthful Disclosures:

Because they are under duress, intimidated, tired, mentally impaired, or confused about their circumstances, suspects may confess to crimes they did not commit.

Using Invalid Forensic Data:

Wrongful convictions can occur when forensic evidence is misleading or inaccurate, sometimes as a result of methods that are obsolete or have flaws.

Defamation or Deception:

Motives such as self-interest, fear of reprisal, or an erroneous assumption of the accused's guilt can lead witnesses to fabricate or mislead testimony.

Incompetent Legal Counsel:

Convictions that are not warranted might occur when defence attorneys are either too busy, too inexperienced, or both.

Misconduct by Prosecutors and Law Enforcement:

Wrongful convictions can result from instances of wrongdoing, including the suppression of exculpatory evidence, the fabrication of evidence, or the coercion of witnesses.

Method for Clearance

Finding Additional Proof:

Evidence of wrongdoing, fresh witness testimony, or DNA evidence may become available that was unavailable during the initial trial.

Evaluate After Conviction:

After receiving fresh evidence, the convicted persons or their legal teams can request a post-conviction review and submit it to the court.

Additional research:

The truth may be revealed through a reinvestigation of the case by groups such as the Innocence Project or by law enforcement.

Process in Court:

Hearings may be scheduled by the court to review the fresh evidence and decide if the conviction ought to be reversed.

Final Ruling:

In light of the new evidence, the court may decide to overturn the conviction and exonerate the person.

Declaration Made Public:

The person is officially cleared of all charges when a formal statement of exoneration is issued.

Personal Effects on the Exoneree and Their Consequences:

Effects on Emotions and Mental Health: PTSD from wrongful imprisonment and other traumatic experiences, as well as difficulties adjusting to life outside of jail, are common mental health issues for exonerees.

Many exonerees confront social reintegration and financial instability, stigma, and a lack of support structures, all after being exonerated.

Salary and Benefits:

Exonerees can seek monetary restitution for the period they spent unlawfully incarcerated under the provisions of certain jurisdictional laws.

Exonerees can get back on their feet with the help of support programs including counselling, job training, and housing subsidies.

Repercussions for the Legal System:

Changes in eyewitness identification protocols, recording of interrogations, and enhancements to forensic methods are all examples of policy reforms that can result from exonerations and work towards the goal of preventing false convictions.

The public may become more cognizant of the shortcomings of the criminal justice system and the necessity of maintaining constant watch to safeguard the innocent when high-profile exonerations take place.

The Innocence Project and Other Prominent Exoneration Groups:

A nonprofit legal group that promotes criminal justice reform and uses DNA evidence to free falsely convicted individuals.

Exonerations Registry at the National Level:

In order to better understand and investigate cases of wrongfully convicted individuals, this joint initiative compiles detailed information regarding all known exonerations in the US.

Conclusion

An essential part of the criminal justice system, exoneration seeks to rectify false convictions and return victims of injustice to their rightful place in society.

Exonerees' emotional, psychological, and financial repercussions underscore the need for comprehensive support and systemic reforms to avoid future injustices, even though new evidence discoveries and the work of organisations committed to this cause are vital.

Exoneration is when someone who was convicted of a crime is found not guilty, either because they proved their innocence or because there was a mistake in the judgement. When someone is on death row, trying to get them released is especially controversial, especially if new proof comes to light after the execution. The transitive word "to exonerate" can also mean to officially clear someone of guilt.

In criminal law, the word "exoneration" also means that a safe bail bond has been paid off and the person is no longer in jail. The judge signs off on the bond, and the clerk of court timestamps the original bail bond power and writes "exonerated" next to it as the judge's order.

Rate of people falsely convicted in the United States of America.

It is not possible to know the exact rate of false convictions in any place, however, often innocent defendants were convicted, all over the country. The rate of false convictions of innocent criminal defendants is unknowable. It is believed that many defendants who received death sentences might be cleared if they receive ongoing legal help over a very long time. Universities in the USA have estimated that between 4 and 12 per cent of all convicted criminal defendants might have been wrongfully convicted.

DNA

The use of DNA can help to exonerate a convicted person. DNA testing done after conviction can help clear the accused. There are many cases where DNA was the reason for the exoneration. Innocence was established in part by post-conviction DNA testing, analysis, or interpretation. It has been used over time to refer to "DNA exoneration". While DNA exonerations have always made up a small percentage of all exonerations, their nature has evolved in terms of the underlying crimes and the significance of non-DNA elements. Most DNA exonerations resulted from sexual assault convictions for which there had been no prior DNA testing. The percentage of erroneous sexual assault convictions that DNA can clear has sharply declined over the years as pretrial DNA testing has become almost standard in rape investigations.

DNA proof is a fairly new way to clear people of crimes. People who had been accused of murder in the United States were first freed because of DNA testing. That person was David Vasquez, who was freed in 1989. Recently, DNA evidence has been used to clear many people who were on death row or serving long jail terms. Since 1999, the number of states letting prisoners ask for DNA tests on their own has grown from two to thirty by October 2003. Access to DNA testing varies a lot by degree, and it can be hard to get tests after a sentence. Groups like the Innocence Project need to free people who were wrongfully convicted based on weak or incorrect proof, even if there is DNA evidence. In some situations, since October 2003, prosecutors must agree to a criminal defendant's request for a DNA test.

Conviction Integrity Units (CIU)

Conviction Integrity Unit (CIU) attempts to stop, recognise, and correct erroneous convictions. Conviction Review Units (CRUs) is another name for them occasionally. Sometimes they function as official committees inside the offices of states or federal solicitors. There is a conviction review process in some smaller offices, but there may not be a formal specialised unit for financial reasons. There has been an increase in the number of Conviction Integrity Units, and several have achieved some success. It is yet unknown if this tendency will result in a general shift in the way prosecutors conduct business.

Compensation

How and by whom are exonerees rewarded is one of the most often asked issues regarding exonerations. People who have been wrongfully convicted can file civil rights and tort cases to get money for their wrongful convictions.

Works Cited

"Department of Justice: Homepage: United States Department of Justice." Department of Justice | Homepage | United States Department of Justice, 2 Aug. 2024, www.justice.gov/.

American Bar Association, www.americanbar.org/. Accessed 7 Aug. 2024.

"Directory of Open Access Journals." DOAJ, www.doaj.org/. Accessed 7 Aug. 2024.

Justia, 22 July 2024, www.justia.com/.

"Project Gutenberg." Project Gutenberg, www.gutenberg.org/. Accessed 7 Aug. 2024.

"Federal Judicial Center." Federal Judicial Center |, www.fjc.gov/. Accessed 7 Aug. 2024.

"New OJP Resources." Office of Justice Programs, www.ojp.gov/ncjrs/new-ojp-resources. Accessed 7 Aug. 2024.

"Research Guides." Home - Research Guides at Harvard Library, guides.library.harvard.edu/. Accessed 7 Aug. 2024.

"Internet Archive: Digital Library of Free & Borrowable Books, Movies, Music & Wayback Machine." Internet Archive: Digital Library of Free & Borrowable Books, Movies, Music & Wayback Machine, archive.org/. Accessed 7 Aug. 2024.

World Legal Information Institute (WorldLII), www.worldlii.org/. Accessed 7 Aug. 2024.

"The Legal Education Foundation." ., thelegaleducationfoundation.org/. Accessed 7 Aug. 2024.

ICC Legal Tools, www.legal-tools.org/. Accessed 7 Aug. 2024.

GovInfo, 1 Aug. 2024, www.govinfo.gov/.

"HathiTrust Digital Library – Millions of Books Online." HathiTrust Digital Library – Millions of Books Online, www.hathitrust.org/. Accessed 7 Aug. 2024.

"Research Guides." Home - Research Guides at Library of Congress, guides.loc.gov/law-library. Accessed 7 Aug. 2024.

"UNODC Publications." United Nations☐:Office on Drugs and Crime, www.unodc.org/unodc/en/publications.html. Accessed 7 Aug. 2024.

"Free Online Course Materials." MIT OpenCourseWare, MIT OpenCourseWare, ocw.mit.edu/. Accessed 7 Aug. 2024.

"Home." Berkeley Law, 7 Aug. 2024, www.law.berkeley.edu/.

"Open Textbook Library." Open Textbook Library, open.umn.edu/opentextbooks. Accessed 7 Aug. 2024.

"Plol☐:The Public Library of Law: Worldcat.Org." OCLC WorldCat.Org, search.worldcat.org/title/PLoL-:-the-public-library-of-law/oclc/228305801. Accessed 7 Aug. 2024.

"Welcome to LII." Legal Information Institute, Legal Information Institute, www.law.cornell.edu/. Accessed 7 Aug. 2024.

www.ingramcontent.com/pod-product-compliance
Lightning Source LLC
Chambersburg PA
CBHW071916210526
45479CB00002B/436